THE BLACK BOOK OF REVENGE

The Complete Manual Of Hardcore Dirty Tricks And Schemes

JOHN JACKSON

Desert Publications

El Dorado, AR 71731-1751 U. S. A.

The Black Book of Revenge

© 1991 by TGS,Inc.

Published by Desert Publications
215 S. Washington
El Dorado, AR 71730
info@deltapress.com

10 9 8 7 6 5 4 3 2
ISBN: 0-87947-167-0
Printed in U. S. A.

Desert Publication is a division of
The DELTA GROUP, Ltd.
Direct all inquiries & orders to the above address.

WARNING NOTICE!

Contents

Author's Note

In this age of advanced communications and ever increasing mobility, it's somewhat difficult to understand that some people never leave the inherent safety of their armchair, and still others never wander past the horizons which they can see from their front porch swing. They sit and watch television, or listen to their favorite radio programs, and such is the extent of their lives. These people are never faced with the need to make decisions pertaining to that which is discussed in this book, for they will always have faith in the system as being designed to protect the rights of the innocent victim. Consequently, this book isn't written for them.

Instead, this book is for those who know what the real world is like. It is written for those who realize that the system is fallible and imperfect at best; corrupt and tainted by dollar signs at worst. It could not have been more succinctly summarized when it was determined in Plato's *Republic* when justice was defined as being "...that which suits the needs of the politically stronger."

And, we know that the terms "politically" and "economically" are essentially interchangeable, so those with the most clout seem to be favored in the current system of justice. In short, this book was written for those who find it expedient to solve their own problems, whatever the consequences may be.

I must include an advanced warning of sorts, however, as this is not a Sunday school book and is quite explicit in detail. The techniques, methods, and tools of the trade are taken from factual instances. They have been used in the past and are still being used on a common basis. These are the tools of revenge.

I would also like to stress that that which is contained herein is depicted solely for the purpose of entertaining reader curiosity and should in no way be used for any purpose(s) where such use is prohibited by law. Furthermore, however simple these devices and techniques may appear, serious personal injury, permanent disfigurement, or even death may result in misapplication. Or worse, the user may find himself caught up in the receiving end of the justice system.

This information is being presented in a manner such that a person having been availed of such knowledge will be better able to protect his family, himself, and his home in a more positive and responsive manner.

Enjoy!

1

Mainframe Thinking

There are many aspects of this subject matter which need to be studied in order for a person to possess a clear and comprehensive understanding of the thought and theory behind the need for retaliatory action. As with most anything, a person must have this keen understanding and awareness and possess a well-informed, working philosophy in order to fully appreciate the art of revenge for its full value and worth. This book, then, will be directed towards the enhancement of a person's individual awareness of the subject of revenge in respect of all its applicable facets. In short, this will be a fairly thorough study of the applicable facets of revenge which require a person to utilize his/her own particular intellect and improvisational talents in order to achieve the desired, optimum effect of the effort expended.

The one most important factor in seeking revenge lies within a person's thinking process by which he will approach his objective. A person must first learn to approach any obstacle with a clear mind and with full and complete understanding of what he is about to undertake. This approach of and focused mental process is called MAINFRAME THINKING.

The psychological reasoning which motivates a person towards seeking revenge is our biological urge which has been termed the SURVIVAL INSTINCT. Essentially, each of us have this inherent drive to survive but because of our upbringing, schooling, social ideals, our individual concepts of morals and ethics tend to undermine this survival drive. We live in a system of social etiquette and therefore allow someone else to represent us and to assist in solving our problems, and we usually fully accept the decision which is then made in these respects. On the other hand, each of us have yet another human trait called FUTILITY, and each person's futility quotient is different. Some people can be pushed and prodded, stomped and dumped upon for an entire lifetime without ever displaying an iota of anger. Others have been known to kill their barber for a bad haircut.

It is our own interpersonal makeup which allows each of us to decide for ourselves what is right or wrong and at what point we're going to draw the line in the sand. This decision to react, which is based upon unique needs, personalities, abilities, and consciences, is where we will begin our study.

This is a decision to modify justice for our own benefit and in most cases, once the decision has been made and the appropriate action taken, the course of action cannot be reversed. Therefore the decision to react must be made with knowledge, insight, and comprehensive understanding of all aspects of the situation that led to the decision to react in the first place. To put it differently, a person should know all of the facts involved in the provocation as well as the reaction in order to be accurately responsive.

1) Before deciding upon any retaliatory action, the strategist would be well advised to know all the facts in the case. The situation should be looked at from all angles of approach and even obscure factors should be examined.

All retaliatory action to a given provocation or argument must be based solely upon the actual facts of the case rather than an imagined or misinterpretation. Unless all of the facts in the case are known, the strategist will sometimes lose a valuable element which could have been used in his favor. Or, if a decision is made on inaccurate information, then the decision itself is erroneous. Take the time to study the situation as well as the target.

The subject of the argument should be understood and the strategist should make all decisions based upon the concerns of the argument itself. Likewise, the subject of the argument should be free from any imagined complications, but all ramifications of responsive action should be considered.

Granted, it is sometimes quite difficult to think a situation through with a clear, analytical process when there is a presence of mental and emotional turmoil, but in order to more fully appreciate the act of revenge, the entire process must be savored like a fine brandy. Only then will the strategist find satisfaction in his actions.

2) Regardless of how asinine this may seem, the basic assumption is that the constitution guarantees equal protection under the law. Therefore, any action the strategist may conceive of (above and beyond assisting the legal system per written ordinance or law) is in effect unlawful and constitutes a crime. So beware.

The basic premise is that two wrongs do not make a right and the justice system is the only entity which is legally capable of making a judgmental determination regarding the punishment of an offender. The parameters with which the strategist must work within must not in any way conflict with the legal system. For the strategist to get caught with his proverbial pants down would be counterproductive to the effort.

A strategist can get caught through any one of the unending barrage of legal entanglements which are all well defined within the volumes of legal statutes which line the walls of our law libraries. Incidentally, these libraries are located in the courthouses in every city and are available to any person who wishes to use them. A well-informed strategist makes full use of these documents in order to clarify any misunderstandings or legal problems he may be involved in or may be involved in at some point in the future. These are the same volumes of legal definitions and statutes from which our attorneys and judges find their seemingly unending line of loop-holes through which the guilty manage to slip.

A strategist can get caught in his operations due to improper planning, over-confidence, or a host of other things which could be detrimental to his success. Suffice it to say that when a strategist becomes overconfident and complacent and stops being just a little paranoid, his chances of being caught increase.

3) The fact that no man is perfect is reflected in the same book that defends the concept of "an eye for an eye." After much and careful consideration of this imperfection, mathematicians have termed this theory as a mathematical law called the HUMAN ERROR FACTOR. By formula, this equates to .07% margin of error in every action or thought that human beings make. This can mean many things, but most importantly it relates to the fact that no matter how well the planning, a strategist's chances of being caught in a "less than legal" situation can never be completely dissolved.

As I pointed out earlier, there are many things which

can cause a strategist to get caught, but some of the more common ones (other than that mentioned earlier) are failure to follow a plan of strategy and not including an escape clause or back-up plan in the offensive action. A strategist should always be careful to plan everything within the scope of operations very thoroughly. Every aspect of the offensive endeavor should be accounted for and properly evaluated in the proper respect of the argument. The strategist should plan as though his very life depends upon the successful execution and completion of the operation, for well it may.

4) In addition to the human error factor, there is a constant and perplexing little creature which is known as HUMAN NATURE, but little more than its actual existence is known. The most precise piece of information about human nature which can be accurately predicted is that human nature cannot be accurately predicted. The person who feels as though he or she can predict and presuppose human nature of even a near-perfect margin, is himself a fool! It is within the capacity of every human being to capriciously change his mind (therefore his destiny) and contrary to the chauvinistic belief, this is not just the prerogative of the female of our species. Because of this quality of unpredictability in human nature, even the best laid plans can result in failure. It should be understood that NO plan should rest entirely upon the supposition of specific actions or responses of another human being. A strategist would do well to learn that he should not ever allow a human being to suffice as an entire link within a chain of execution.

This is not to say that the human element should be excluded form the chain, simply that uncertainty and precaution should be factors which sort of overview the tactical planning stages of the operation. A back-up or alternate plan of action should remain ever in focus to be readily implemented should the initial plan become a potential pitfall.

It should be remembered that any chain is only as strong as its weakest link, and the weak link can result in anything from a simple failure to a reversal of player components where the strategist becomes the target.

5) A rose is a rose, etc, unless it smells like doggie dung. The concept of tact, cunning, and con-artistry can be possibly the most important commodities that a strategist can have in his/her bag of tricks. If the strategist has the gift of gab, an honest twinkle in the eye, and a splash of sincere believability, it has been said that he can sell the Brooklyn Bridge. If he is cunning and well versed in the art of conning, he can sell the Eiffel Tower to the US President.

Tact has been defined as the ability to look someone in the eye, tell the person to go to hell, and in such a manner as to cause the person to smile, whistle a tune, and feel totally content as he strolls along his merry way towards the fiery gates of purgatory.

However, as the saying goes: "you can't bullshit a bullshitter!" There is always a person who lurks about who is either a bigger con, a more believable bullshitter, or who is simply a helluva lot luckier. On the opposite extreme, a word of caution comes from the man who has worn so many masks in his lifetime that he lost track of who he really was. He simply got lost in the shuffle.

6) Some people are blessed with vernacular where others are blessed with good looks or money. And every now and again you cannot avoid running across that

simple soul who has a guardian angel resting upon his shoulders. In this case, problems will roll off him like water off the back of a duck. The harder things hit him, the stronger and more resilient he becomes.

This type of person is a strong adversary but a point must be understood: every person alive has their little weak spot, just as each has their own skeletons in their closets. If the weak spot or skeleton can be located, the target can be managed with little or no effort, and without fail.

7) Know yourself as well as your strengths and weaknesses. Know your good points, bad points, proficiencies, and limitations. This type of knowledge can only come from complete and impartial, truthful self-analysis which is called INTROSPECTION.

You should never go fishing for shark unless you know what to do with one if you should hook one. To be succinct, you should never start something that you can't handle or cannot bring to a favorable conclusion. This is a lesson which should be learned from within the safety of the armchair rather than on the battlefield.

8) Once a plan has been put into action, there are always trace remnants from the path of progression. Be sure that whatever the plan of attack is, it involves an alternative for covering tracks.

It's the same as having fired a weapon in that several things can occur:

a) There is absolutely no control of the projectile once it departs the muzzle of the weapon. The strategist must be sure of his target and equally sure that no-one is going to inadvertently step in between himself and his target. Also, the path of the projectile isn't necessarily complete once the target has been hit. If the projectile was too overpowering, it will pass through the target and possibly hit an innocent bystander in the process of progression. Therefore, the complete path of the projectile should be known before the trigger is ever pulled.

b) Once a weapon has been fired, there exists something known as the SMOKING GUN, and possession there-of constitutes very severe legal difficulties!

c) Whenever anything is touched by the strategist, it should be remembered that fingerprints are the signature of the strategist's conscience.

These generalizations can be applied to many things other than the firing of a gun. In any case, they constitute truths and should not be overlooked nor taken lightly. A strategist should always be certain of all the ramifications of his actions and should likewise be prepared for any reaction. One other thing: the bigger the gun, the harder the kick! If a strategist can't handle the recoil he should use a smaller weapon.

9) There exists a physical law (thanks, Isaac Newton) which states that, for every action there is an equal and opposing reaction. Put into street terminology: what goes around, comes around. The strategist should realize that there is going to be an opposite action to every item of his plan.

10) Everyone has a person or two he can trust with his most deepest, darkest secrets. This may be a wife, a date mate, a lover, or just a good friend. In any case, it's not always very wise to share everything with a friend. If a strategist doesn't want a secret to be told then he should not have told it in the first place. Just as the strategist has someone he can trust with HIS secrets, so has the person he trusted. Again, it's not just the prerogative of

the female to gossip and share some juicy piece of information. Some of the most interesting tidbits of information I have ever picked up came from male lawyers who just happened to be sitting in a near-by booth or table at a restaurant I frequent.

It's really easy to see that a person who is a staunch friend or supporter can quickly become a fierce member of the opposition. Nothing is forever (except death and taxes) and the secret you share now may soon become the ammunition that hits you in the future. It's stupid to give away ammunition, unless the ammo is booby-trapped, armed with a self-destruct mechanism, or is relatively useless and used to judge the strength of the relationship.

Remember that human nature is subject to change in the blink of an eye, a mood swing, or on a whim. A strategist should always keep an open mind and never turn his back upon an enemy (unless, of course, he has a death-wish!)

11) A strategist should always know his surroundings and be able to blend well within any environment. He should always keep his bearings (and perspective) as well as a keen and cool wit. He should remember the premise of "hide in plain sight" and be able to do just that. He should be able to rely on each of his senses individually as well as read the correlated information which his brain files on an average of a thousand times per second.

In more common terms, when in Rome, do as the Romans do. The concept may sound easy but can be quite difficult to master. However, practice makes perfect. If the plan is critical and the desired outcome constitutes something less that lawful, there is no room for doubt or mistakes.

12) I cannot stress enough the need for careful situational analysis and for planning and strategy. Careful analysis will make the difference between the success or failure of a plan, and how a strategist perceives the world around him will determine the correctness or incorrectness of his analysis.

That device situated between your ears (the thing we call a brain) can only synthesize and correlate information which the host human allows to be perceived or processed. We can only process intelligence if we keep and maintain an open mind and allow ourselves to fully appreciate our full compliment of sensory gathering devices. As the information is processed, intelligence is further heightened by allowing free-flowing thought called imagination. The difference between possible and impossible lie within the limits of our imagination.

It's only when a person puts to use the combination of insight, sensory awareness, and acquired skills that he becomes more intelligent. As he learns to put to use this new-found intelligence in real-life situations that his intelligence turns to wisdom. And, as he learns restraint, reasoning, and other such factors, his wisdom increases. Many people know how to accomplish a task with effectiveness and efficiency, but it's only a wise person who actually knows what the hell is going on in the first place.

It's not the goal of this book to make philosophers or wise sages of everyone who feels the need for a little home-grown justice. In the successive chapters, there will be a few philosophical quotes, perhaps an axiom or two, but only to broaden the reader's perspective and open up the imagination. In many instances, it is required that a strategist be spontaneous and adaptable but in order to be either, he has to have a fertile imagination and can see things for their potential or possibilities as well as for what they actually are. It is to stimulate reader focus upon the possibilities which surround us and lie deep within us as we face our points of futility and reach deep within ourselves for the answers to our problems. Without a stimulated and fertile imagination, we might as well turn over our rights to the attorneys and judges who fight to control the rights of the people in the first place, then assume the position in the armchair with not so much as a word of displeasure when an injustice occurs.

The most important thing to start the imagination churning away is to realize that there is an imperfection within everyone. The strategist must strive for perfection while searching for the target's imperfection, which when found can then be dealt with in a constructive manner (destructively speaking.)

Henry David Thoreau was quoted as having said that "Time is the stream I go a'fishin' in." I think he was referring to the fact that we can do whatever we desire with the time we have allotted, except for lengthening it. Life is short and each person shouldn't reduce his allotment by unforeseen and careless screw-ups.

2

Three Approaches

In an offensive situation there are three approaches or specific areas of target vulnerabilities: mental, physical, and emotional. These are categorized for the purposes of strategy delineation and tactical planning. Regardless of the particular type of offensive measure, the general thrust or operational strike towards a particular target should take the following course:

1) Isolation of target. The target must be specifically recognized and the central focus of the operational plan.

2) Information procession. A complete and comprehensive study of the target must be made so that all variables and contingencies are fully recognized and understood. This includes the target's personal habits, lifestyle, personality, environment, and any other facets which may ultimately affect the outcome of the tactical offensive. It should also be stressed that ALL variables should be considered for their potential strengths and weaknesses and then each compared to the other on a scale of evaluation.

At this point, the strategist should rate his own strengths and weaknesses against those of the target to get an insight of differences which might be used in the planning stages of the operation.

3) Planning/Strategy. This stage is extremely important and it should be noted that all information which is subject for utilization within tactical operations should

be clear and concise (as well as precise.) If any variable goes unresearched, the extent of the offensive based upon that particular contingency will remain vague, or unclear, and erroneous information may be extrapolated and used which could result in negative consequences for the strategist.

Realize that the best laid plans are often the simplest ones. If the offensive is complicated and mentally distracting, the strategist may become too involved in the operation and lose his perspective. In law enforcement circles, the key is to keep all operations exactly as you would want a woman's skirt to be: short, brief, and with interesting prospects.

Naturally, the planning stage is the most critical because it's where all the information is brought together and correlated, then a package of logistics is squeezed from the mixture. These logistics are then re-scrutinized one more time for flaws before being put into actual operation.

4) Attack. This is the physical follow-up of all the prior stages of planning. The attack should run on schedule and if there is any appreciable deviation from the plan, the operation should be scrapped and the back-up or contingency plan immediately implemented. Note that the alternate plan of attack should blend with the original plan so as not to cause too much disruption in the process of switching from one plan to the next.

5) Evaporate. This is exactly as it sounds: get out; leave; disappear; vanish. The strategist, upon completion of the operation, should immediately resume a normal lifestyle as though absolutely nothing has occurred. If it was normal for the strategist to be pissed off at the target, a change in attitude or emotion would stick

out like a sore thumb! And while it's normal human nature to want to return to the scene of the "crime", the strategist would be well advised to rely upon his keen sense of planning and imagine the outcome as being nothing more or less than the desired outcome of the operation. If there is any unusual occurrence, in due time the strategist will find out about it through normal course of events. On the other hand, it wouldn't hurt to at least keep an ear tuned to the local gossip-line in the event something went awry and he decides there might be a need to take a vacation in another country for a while! These approaches and strategies should be recognized and utilized in all offensive operations. The exact strategy depends upon the desired outcome of the operation, the capabilities of the strategist, what is made possible by the variables of the target, and the resources available to the strategist.

The method of approach depends upon the target's accessibility or approachability as well as the strategist's desired outcome of the operation. For example: the target may not be approachable on a physical level, but accessible on a mental or emotional level. The plan, then, would be to proceed with whatever would suit the needs of the strategist from that particular level.

On the other hand, if all three avenues of approach are of equal avail to the strategist, he must then choose one which meet the criteria of simplicity and goal attainment. He must correlate the information so that he can conclude the course of action in the minimal occurrence of time and maximum efficiency of the tactical design.

Whatever the course of action, the strategy should be carefully adhered to and within close tolerances. Spontaneous and unrequired improvisation should be left for brain-games for the strategist's imagination. A fully operational escape clause or bail-out plan must always remain on the back burner, left to simmer so that spontaneous improvisation isn't necessary.

MENTAL APPROACH

There are many aspects to this avenue of approach but this basically refers to any definitive action which creates any adverse effect upon the target. This type of action does not create a physical link between the strategist and the target. This creates an effect upon the target which is more implied or inferred from the circumstances and the target should not be able to physically see or feel the result of the offensive. In other words, mental harassment would be an example of the mental approach.

As well, the positive qualities of this approach may overshadow the negative qualities (respective of the target) even to the extent of the negativities appearing to be nothing more than a minor human error factor.

The offensive may be the utilization of many techniques from mild to extreme action against the target to tactical efforts which result in the complete mental breakdown and collapse of the target. Most often, the desired effects of the offensive operation result in general mental anguish of the target through the loss of family or peer respect, loss of credibility or standing in the community, family, or work place, enhanced paranoia, mental conflict within himself, or a total loss of social standing.

There are many methods to achieve the desired effects but the strategist should bear in mind that the technique chosen should depend largely upon the target's individual stress point to the extent that the target should be able to feel an adverse "force" working against him but cannot distinguish from where it's coming.

Sensory adaptation is the psychological term which refers to a person's adaptation to certain environmental stressors. This describes the target's state of perception after having been exposed to an external stimulus which evokes or elicits pain, stress, mental tension, or alters a person's perception of his environment. For instance, a subject who experiences constant physical pain such as a headache or throbbing backache for a lengthy period of time, with no relief from the stimulus, the pain is perceived by the target as having become more generalized and decreasing in intensity. As constant exposure of the subject to the pain stimulus becomes generalized, the pain creates a mental immunity (of sorts) to similar pain of lesser intensity thus allowing the subject to adapt to the stimulus. This negates the lasting effects of impressions of this type of stimulus. For this approach to be workable, the strategist would have to make certain that the pain or mental stimulus was upgraded or intensified on a regular interval else the target will adapt and work around it.

If a person is exposed to a stimulus which causes a variance of mental irritability, the change in his presence of mind may not allow him to successfully cope with his normal everyday pressures. He may, in this state of mind, be vulnerable to associative mental stressors which would otherwise be a normal part of his daily routine. In either case, the offensive irritation should be monitored and the intensity upgraded or heightened or all stressors will be generalized and adapted.

The success of the operation under the mental approach depends upon being able to upset the target's mental equilibrium to the extent of extreme mental reaction to minor, predetermined stressors. The strategist must be careful no to allow the offensive being overshadowed by the target's pre-existing environmental clutter (the natural events which occur within a person's life through normal environmental exposure.) A strategist should also realize that the amplification of a target's naturally occurring environmental clutter can be effectively increased or changed by the addition of new stressors. This will cause the target to view his most mundane stressor as a new and unmanageable irritant.

The important factor is that once the target attains a state of mental equilibrium, he may recognize things which are not of the normal course of his routine and may even begin to deduce that the additional clutter is of other than accidental occurrences. Once he determines that the amplified stressors are of an artificial design or otherwise invoked by a human endeavor, he will then be able to cope against further thrusts and may even be able to determine the source of the harassment. If the target is allowed to regroup and think things through, he may even be able to critically analyze the situation and redirect the exact course of the offensive so that it returns to its point of origin.

Although techniques should be more or less custom tailored to the target and the occasion, some examples of successful methods and techniques are as follows.

If a person has recently experienced a death in the family, a very debilitating maneuver on the strategist's part would be to send the target daily successive deliveries of black wreaths, or even "get well" cards, or "wish you were here" cards being addressed from the deceased. This can cause rather traumatic anguish. The operation should not be carried to the extent that the strategist lose sight of the original goal, however. If the latter occurs, the strategist would probably be apprehended by the law enforcement agencies but would not be held as there are no laws which govern bad taste.

Some strategists may be opposed to this type of morbid deviousness, even though, he should understand that sardonically motivated acts play upon the target causing great stress, especially when used concurrently with other methods.

On a less morbid note, we can also direct efforts towards other aspects of the target's lifestyle. If a target has an answering machine, the strategist should note that preplanned "messages" can be left on the target's machine to put a particular point across. The equipment needed includes a portable tape recorder, a telephone pickup microphone, a few blank tapes, and the phone numbers of several mortuaries.

Basically, the strategist only has to dial the number of the first mortuary on his list and record the greeting from the establishment: "Hello. This is Jerk-o's Funeral Home. How may I be of service?"

The strategist would then proceed down the list of mortuary phone numbers until he has recorded several business greetings which would be replayed into the target's answering machine. It comes as somewhat of a shock for someone to check the messages on a machine to find that he has been besieged by a barrage of mortuaries wanting to be of service to him!

As an interjection at this point, it might be well to inform the potential strategist that some states are currently experimenting with a new telephone system which enables the called party to see the number of the phone he is being called from by an led display on his equipment. But pay phones aren't that expensive, especially if the target's telephone credit card number can be obtained and used. This would sort of make it appear that the target is calling himself.

In some instances, it really doesn't matter whether or not the target has an answering machine as it is always good if there is no evidence to substantiate the target's claims of harassment. The mortuary messages can simply be played directly to the target as he answers his phone. When this technique is used with the black wreath or occasion card, the target becomes quite emotionally distraught and tends to lose his edge on reality.

A variation on this theme would be effective if the strategist happened to find out that the target were having an adulterous affair. The spouse of the target's lover could be verbally provoked and the response then recorded ("You son of a bitch! When I get my hands on you I'll rip your fucking heart out!"), then played back over the phone to the target. This works even better when the target is in the company of his lover. This type of harassment has been known to destroy what otherwise would have been a fruitful affair.

There are virtually thousands of answering-machine variations which can be used to mentally harass a target. Such as recording the target's machine greeting and playing it back as a message into his system. When the target checks his machine for messages he will be quite surprised to find his greeting being played and will quickly think that his machine is not operating properly. This works well if the "message" is played into the target's machine a few times a day for a week or so.

As an interjection, the strategist can make use of a similar system for a call-screening capabilities on his own answering machine. Acquisition of a telephone company prerecorded message (out of order, changed number, not a working number, etc.) can be found quite easily, recorded on a portable tape recorder, then played into the strategist's machine as his greeting. A caller who isn't familiar with the set up will immediately come to the conclusion that the message was a bona-fide phone company recording and will probably not call back. However, a person who has been forewarned of the message will simply wait for the recording to finish then leave his message at the customary beep. This works well to stop bill collectors, ex-spouses, etc. from constantly calling and leaving harassing messages on the strategist's machine.

The telephone is a very insidious device on a psychological level due to the fact that it allows a stranger to enter your house. A person's personal space can then be violated, if only verbally, and thus leaving the owner of the phone to feel somewhat violated as well. The system of call screening allows the strategist to essentially have an unreachable phone number on a moment's notice and little (if any) expense.

The answering machine isn't germane to the expedience of these tactics but allows a buffer zone between the target and strategist. On the other hand, if the target were a drug dealer, for example, the last thing in the world he would want to hear would be the sounds of police radios crackling over an otherwise silent phone line, especially if he answers his phone in the middle of a transaction. Likewise, a narcotics agent would feel less than secure if he were to receive a phone call which transmitted the sounds of a known drug hot spot such as an arcade or night club.

In any case, the desired effect is to mentally unravel the target or cause some sort of mental stress aimed at the deterioration of the target's feeling of security, both physically as well as mentally.

Another approach is to destroy the credibility of the target with his (assuming that the target is a male) wife, which does not necessarily depend upon the fact of the target being unfaithful. Situations can present themselves in various ways and can quickly erode all credibility given the target by his spouse.

The strategist would need the assistance of a willing female accomplice to start the ball rolling. The accomplice would wait for the target to get off from work, for instance in an office building, then casually but literally bump into him in a crowd or elevator. In the contact, a bit of cheap perfume could be "accidentally" spilled onto the target, and if the accomplice is skilled she can even manage to smudge her lipstick upon the target's shirt during the bump. The accomplice disappears and the target heads for home. When he enters his home, his spouse will undoubtedly question him about the lipstick and perfume to which he would tell the truth (as he honestly knew it.)

A few days later, a pair of panties could be placed beneath the seat of the target's automobile, a tube of lipstick placed into the crack of the front seat, and perfume (preferably the kind which was used in the bumping incident) sprayed into the car's interior. The target's wife will invariably find the smells in the car (even if she has to be alerted by a "jealous husband" calling to leave a warning for her to keep her husband from his wife) and then the items will be found, and hell hath no fury as the attorney of a woman scorned! Even if the target somehow managed to successfully squirm out of the indictment of his wife, his original credibility will have been shattered. Further attacks by the strategist would be devastating as the wife would be suspicious from that time forward.

The target is now in a "no win" situation. Legitimate wrong number phone calls late in the night, coming home late from work for legitimate reasons, or other such things will tend to provoke disparity between the target and his wife.

These techniques work without fail when put into use, and work even better when several techniques are used successively. This can cause mental, and depending upon the temper of the target's spouse or lover, can cause physical distress as well.

Something else which would cause the disturbance of an individual's credibility (especially among people in the office) would be to purchase a magazine subscription in the target's name which immediately contradicts his lifestyle. This subscription could be forwarded to his place of business and could create havoc. For example, a gay periodical sent to a school teacher or city employee, or a communistic magazine sent to a government, military, or defense contractor. The latter would not only place the target in a precarious position with his peer group but would also cause him to be temporarily suspended from work and would cause his name to be placed on a "hot list" by agencies such as the CIA, FBI, and the highly secret NSA. A government employee's entire future is immediately jeopardized.

Rumors can be another avenue by which the strategist can retaliate against a chosen target. I am reminded of one case in particular where the manager of an apartment complex, a divorced middle aged lady, constantly harassed her tenants pertaining to things which she had no right getting involved in. If a tenant fought the issue, it would be certain there would be an eviction to settle the dispute, or the tenant would be harassed into leaving the complex. This went on until the manager began to harass a young female who had the presence of mind to remedy the situation. After reaching her point of futility, the strategist attempted to settle matters through the proper channels but found no legal recourse. She decided to handle matters in her own unique way.

After doing her homework and researching the apartment manager's background, she finally decided upon a course of action which pertained to the fact that the manager had previously lost a similar job due to drinking (remember about the skeletons in the closet?). After she formulated her plan and gathered her "tools", she sat back and waited until she knew she could implement her system with no difficulty or chance of being found out.

Then she slipped into action. She had been collecting beer cans—one brand—and on the night prior to the apartment manager's monthly inspection by the property management group, the strategist tossed several of the empty cans into the apartment manager's car, onto her patio, and even managed to get a few into the waste basket inside the manager's office, then left the basket in plain sight of anyone who happened to venture into the office.

The next morning, the property was inspected by the

supervisor who found the beer cans almost immediately. Of course, the apartment manager didn't know anything about them and explained that fact to her bosses. Reluctantly, they agreed to overlook the incident, but again, there was a substantial loss of credibility for the manager.

The strategist then began watching for the manager to bring in her weekly supply of beer from the store. After giving the manager time to consume several cans of the beverage (it was Friday night, and it was found to be sort of a weekly thing for the manager to have a few too many almost every Friday night) then made a phone call to the local police department. Feigning slurred speech, she identified herself as the apartment manager then proceeded to give the police dispatcher a complaint that there were several residents who were in violation of an excessive noise ordinance.

The police officers were sent to the scene, checked extensively around the complex but found no signs of a disturbance. The officers then approached the manager's apartment and found her to be considerably less than sober. They noted in their report that the call was obviously made by an intoxicated person.

The strategist began slipping beer cans into the manager's car from time to time when no-one was looking, and even managed to place a few more in the office without being discovered. Then it began to be noticed by the other tenants that there seemed to be an excessive amount of cans strewn about, indicating (although circumstantially) that the manager was consuming an abundance of alcohol. A call was made by a tenant, being placed to the property management group, notifying them of the situation. This call was not made by the strategist, and when the supervisors came to inspect the complex, she was just completing another placement of cans. The supervisors thought she was cleaning them up, however, and even commended her for taking an active part in her concern for the complex.

Due to the fact that not only had several tenants complained about the manager but the police department had complained as well, the manager was dismissed from her job. The strategist never received another complaint while she was at the complex.

Another situation comes to mind where the strategist "borrowed" a bicycle from another tenant and placed it on the apartment manager's upstairs balcony. How he got it there I'll never know because the balcony was only accessible from inside the apartment. Regardless, a stolen bicycle report was made to the police department.

Upon arrival at the complex, the officers took a look around and found the bicycle. They queried the manager as to how it got on his balcony and as they were listening to his feeble explanation, one of the officers happened to notice the familiar odor of marijuana coming from within the apartment. Consequently the man lost his job as well as his freedom, being incarcerated on charges of possession of a controlled substance.

The loss of credibility can be a very hard thing to cope with and although the loss can sometimes be overcome, the experience can be a lasting memory.

As the strategist researches his target, he may find weaknesses or past indiscretions which may make his strike against the target easier than expected. He may find that his target has already experienced a substantial loss of credibility from other instances which still plague the target which can be re-ignited into a roaring blaze with little or no actual effort other than a strategically placed telephone call or a well written letter, either of which directed to a person who has some sort of control over the target.

Thus, it is most helpful to the strategist if he or she is able to secure personal information about the intended target. Info such as social security numbers, date of birth, drivers' license information, family information, as well as information relating to close friends and/or the spouse of the target. You can tell a lot about a target by checking to see who his friends AND enemies are, and information in either case may prove invaluable later on down the road.

As an example of the availability of information relating to the target, if the strategist contacts the Social Security Administration with a money order for (at the time of this writing, $8.00), he will be made available all of the target's employment history, government status relating to employability, nationality, age, etc. Of course, when contacting the federal government it is not usually too very wise to offer as a stated reason for requesting such information as being, "This person is a potential target for vengeful retaliatory action!" As a matter of fact, it has been said that the government generally DOES NOT CHECK TO SEE IF THE INFORMATION THEY SEND OUT IN RESPONSE TO SUCH A REQUEST ACTUALLY GOES TO THE PERSON WHO ACTUALLY REQUESTED THE INFORMATION, A PROSPECTIVE EMPLOYER, ETC.

Along the same lines, but varying from state to state, one can also receive a target's drivers' license history which relates to accidents, moving violations, restrictions on driving privileges and the reasons for such restrictions (alcoholism, drug/substance dependency, insanity, etc.) However, it would behoove the strategist to check with the laws of each state regarding the legal requirements for obtaining such information. Most states are somewhat more cautious about who they send such information to.

With this minimal information the strategist has acquired, much can be accomplished such as accessing a target's credit report, interrupting utility services (gas, electricity, water, telephone, etc.), or efforts as such are limited by the strategist's imagination. In one situation, I can imagine using such information, and of course the target's name, in calling the target's phone company and requesting that (the target's) phone service be interrupted, terminated, or changed with the new number being unlisted and not available to anyone except in person at the phone company office. Of course, it would be wise, I imagine, for a strategist to be absolutely certain that the target cannot be reached by the phone company to verify such a request. In the event that he is not reached, the request will be honored.

Bear in mind that this type of service interruption is very distressing and will cause much anguish for the target, especially if the service is manipulated on a Friday (for it will be Monday before it can be returned to normal), and would be especially harassing if it were to occur just prior to a long, holiday week-end. The lengthened wait in repairing the "problem" greatly adds to the anger and increases the target's hostility towards the phone company for allowing their "screw-up" to have occurred in the first place! I know I'd be pretty darned miffed! And, the service is eventually corrected, unless the target is in arrears on his bill, in which case he must bring his account to date before other action on his account can be taken (except permanent disconnection!)

To further illustrate the hazards of having personal information fall into the wrong hands, I will illustrate yet another scenario which affects a target's mail service. On a Thursday afternoon, a strategist strolled into a post office, filled out a change of address card and dropped it in the "local" mail slot. Within a couple of days, the target's mail service was halted and effectively re-routed to another location (which could have been any city or state in which the target did not reside). And, the government is notorious for it's slow service and response to problems, consequently it took over a month and a half to have this one corrected! This worked due to the fact that a person no longer has to be physically present for mail service to be altered or stopped, and in this case the guilty party was never found because there was no way to identify the responsible party.

An ironic twist to this is when mail is re-routed to the target's enemies, or the strategist can direct hits on two targets simply by having mail from one target directed to the other and at the same time vice versa. Or, the mail of a target (hypothetically a person with less than scrupulous character) directed to the local narcotics officer or gossip columnist.

These are simply examples of the endless possible methods of retaliation under the mental approach. In summarizing this approach, the overall intent is to cause the target mental anguish and inflict mental distress through any tactic which can be conceived of in which the strategist does not have to physically confront the target, or even be anywhere near the target for the operation to be successful. To be sure, a wise strategist will locate the target's potential weaknesses, strengths, and examine his mind for any method which would cause considerable turmoil in the target's life, then the strategist will exploit such weaknesses to whatever ends necessary to achieve a desired effect or predetermined offensive goal. At this point, we shall move on to the Physical Approach.

PHYSICAL APPROACH

This particular alternative action approach presents a core element of danger to the strategist in that he/she more physically participates in the action, and that the action is to be directed at the target's physical well-being. In this approach, there are no barriers of anonymity as seen in the previous approach and the strategist himself may be placed in danger of detection (which is sometimes very counterproductive to the effort!) Another ramification to consider is the fact that the end result, being physically manifested against the target and possibly causing him harm, there is a clear legal definition which can be anything from terroristic threats to attempted and/or pre-meditated murder. Consequently, the assessment of the outcome of the operation will be easier to present in a court of law, and to a jury who probably would not see the validity in the strategist's actions (depending upon who the target is, of course, the strategist may get a commendation!) It should be stressed, and the strategist should take heed to this notice, that all factors and variables in the planned operation must be very carefully weighed against the motivational factors as well as the desired outcome of such operations!

Although there are several classifications within this approach, let's examine only two in this chapter, with the possibility of addendum elsewhere in the book. The two we'll look at are General Physical Harassment and Basic Confrontation Tactics (with anonymity as a focus where possible.)

The thought behind the physical harassment is for the strategist to utilize whatever techniques and tactics (or devices or equipment) to bring about an optimal conclusion to planned operations. The fundamental idea is to keep the offensive action as simple as possible while inflicting the maximum amount of destruction (although not necessarily physical destruction). This is exemplified by the activities of the Ku Klux Klan in the early South: burnt crosses in the yards of their enemies, the painting of crosses and symbols upon front doors, symbolic hangings (in effigy), and being able to get to those who were thought to be untouchable. Their basic strategy was two-fold and very simple.

First, their approach was to divide and conquer. In realizing that there is strength in numbers, they would locate a potential target and strike at a location and at such a time as to find the target alone or otherwise outnumbered by the Klan.

Secondly, the Klan sought to put real fear behind their name so that whoever heard the name mentioned would immediately recognize it as something which represented strength and action. This was accomplished by recruiting members of professions which would perpetuate the Klan's activities. Their masses would form in great numbers and in secrecy so that outsiders would not know the identities of those in the organization.

Their efforts were extremely successful and depending

upon which side of the fence a person stands on, the Klan (to this day) can be a very capable ally or a very strong adversary.

The next case we'll look at involves the correction of the justice deficit which remained after a young female was struck and killed by an intoxicated driver. Although the driver was apprehended, and was a repeat offender of driving while intoxicated, he was allowed to plead guilty to the charge of disorderly conduct with a motor vehicle. Because he was apprehended while standing outside his vehicle and there was no witness to the killing, it was more or less assumed that he, being drunk, was guilty. He confessed to the crime while he was still drunk and the confession was thrown out by the judge as inadmissible evidence. The driver, knowing that he had met with great fate, decided not to push things and was allowed to bargain his way out of the system. Of course there were some repercussions: he was put on probation for five years and his drivers' license was suspended for three years (except for the purposes of driving to and from work, church, and home.)

This miscarriage of justice was substantially more than the father could take, and since he had no action in the case whatsoever (the case being prosecuted by the state) there was nothing that he could do to change or even appeal the ruling. He knew, however, that he would not, could not let it end there with his daughter lying dead at the hands of a man who had no remorse for his crime. He knew that he would find a way to at least partially put matters into correct perspective!

The grieving father began to research the man who was responsible for his little girl's death, and soon learned his habits, favorite night spots, and the noontime "watering holes" he frequented on a regular basis. He learned, too, that his target's probation was as much of a joke as all other facets of the ruling, and further that the target had himself once been a law enforcement officer but had to resign his position due to the inability to handle the stress of the job.

The strategist took this information home and studied it for several days, mulling over the possibilities in his mind. He memorized times, locations, names, and the face that he killed over and over in his dreams.

He awoke in the middle of the night in a cold sweat and it suddenly occurred to him how he could get his revenge and be rid of his target and tormentor once and for all. The next evening, and for several evenings to follow, the strategist began to sit among the ranks of those at the target's favorite night spot. He would sit quietly, listen to the brash country music, suffer through the smoke-filled room, and sip his Coca-Cola, savoring not only the sweet taste of the soda-pop but the taste of revenge, as well, which was now close at hand.

Then the night arrived. He squinted his eyes against the haze of the room and from across the dance floor, sitting undiscernibly in the shadows, he watched his target down glass after glass of beer, chasing every other glass with a shot of Kentucky bourbon. Hours passed before the target even began showing the slightest signs of intoxication yet the strategist maintained his patience. He sat at his table with an ever-increasing fire in his eyes, mind, and heart.

The last call for alcohol came about and all of the club patrons were quickly hustled out the door, left to stagger to their vehicles in the parking lot. The target was by now somewhat less than in a sober condition. He approached his car and fumbled for his keys for several minutes before finally finding the one that would unlock the door. He started the engine and pulled slowly onto the highway, the strategist following behind but not suspiciously close. They drove down the highway in darkness for what seemed like an eternity before the strategist was finally able to make his move.

The strategist began to close the distance between their vehicles while making certain that the highway was deserted. He pulled his car into the lane next to the target's car and slowly, nervously, reached to the seat where he picked up a high-intensity automotive spotlight which had been rebuilt to house a strobe bulb instead of the normal flood light. He carefully aimed the device at the target, tapped his horn, and as the target turned his head towards the strategist the strobe was switched on, momentarily blinding the target. The strategist had planned this maneuver well and had carried it out in his mind at least a thousand times, so he knew by instinct the exact location in which he would need to switch the light on in order to blind the target for just the amount of time that it would take for him to miss a fairly sharp curve in the highway. The plan was executed without flaw and the strategist pulled his car to a stop as he watched the lights of the target's car disappear over the side of the cliff. He thought to himself that it was strange that the car didn't burst into flames as it hit bottom a few hundred feet below. But, he was satisfied that the target would never again be allowed to kill, and the little girl's death was finally avenged.

In related instances, there have been grapevine reports of "bump-and-rob" which are aimed at intoxicated drivers who have been staked out in night clubs and other drinking establishments. It is said that these in-ebriated drivers are tailed from these locations and when they come to a deserted spot on the road, they are bumped into with another vehicle and more-or-less forced to stop on the road side. At this point, the intoxicated driver is approached where-by one of several things can happen. The victim is either outright robbed and forced to drink even more liquor, then is found by a law enforcement officer who summarily takes him to jail while refusing to listen to the drunken claims and allegations of being robbed and forced to get drunk. Even if there was an investigation, it would be found that the victim had just left a club in a drunken condition.

Or, the strategist will simply acknowledge that the accident was in fact his own fault and even offers to call the police or highway patrol. At this point, the victim becomes very concerned about the possibility of going to jail for driving while intoxicated. He offers to pay for the repair of the strategist's automobile, or even offers a greater monetary incentive. He may realize that he has been sucker-punched, but the lesser of the two evils in a case such as this would be the involvement of a cop.

The strategist always accepts the money, and one in particular even donates his proceeds to a very active group to help fight the battle against drunk drivers. And while others donate their proceeds to charitable organizations, there are still some who simply reap the benefits for their efforts.

In cases such as these, the strategists plan their moves well and stake out establishments which are frequented by persons who tend to carry substantial amounts of cash on their persons. The strategist doesn't have to rely upon human nature or the buffer of anonymity (who's going to call the police in the first place?) and the target is going to be the one who is in immediate violation of the law. The plan is relatively safe, simple, and can prove to be very rewarding.

In another case which involved an intoxicated target, the strategist was a neighbor who found his automobile vandalized and his dog attacked by the target who went into a usual violent rage with no provocation. As in other cases, charges were pressed but the fine was light. The victim had had enough!

The belligerent drunk had, in this case, picked on the wrong person.

Being the next door neighbor of the target, the strategist had almost no difficulty in finding the target's weak spot: an almost phobic fear of snakes.

The target and strategist lived in a somewhat rural setting and there was about a half of a mile of field and wooded area between their houses. There were no other houses in the immediate area, so there was no immediate concern for the target pertaining to witnesses and his offensive strike would be easily staged.

The strategist began collecting snakes from the local creeks, streams, and stock-tanks, storing them in 55-gallon drums inside his garage, waiting for right moment. He began to closely watch his target to observe patterns within his lifestyle. He found that his target would leave the house the same time every morning, he would return home the same time each evening. On Fridays, the target would stop off from work and spend a few hours at the local bar where he would invariable get stone drunk and proceed to cause problems for everyone he came into contact with. The strategist also found that the back door of the target's house was generally left unlocked, which was not an unusual occurrence in such a small town.

One Friday morning, the strategist moved into action. He collected his snakes and put them into burlap bags and when the target left for work he slipped into the back door. He strategically placed the slippery serpents throughout the entire house: in the cupboards, the food pantry, beneath the cushions on the sofa, between the mattress and bed sheets, in the toilet bowl, and even in the medicine cabinet. He slipped back home and waited, knowing that he wouldn't have long to wait.

The strategist waited for a few days and it suddenly occurred to him that he had heard nothing which would indicate that his offensive was successful, but he quickly realized that neither had he seen his "neighbor" around town or even at home. The town folks had missed him as well and the strategist soon found that the target had not been to work since that Friday.

The next day, the strategist decided that he had to feed his curiosity. He strolled down the road to the target's house, only to find that the house had been vacated. As he stood on the porch, a car pulled into the driveway bearing the name of a local real estate company. After speaking to the agent, the strategist found that the target had indeed left for greener, and less snakier, pastures, leaving behind the dishes in the cupboards, food in the pantry, the mattresses, and other things in which the snakes had been in contact with.

The strategist also found that the Realtor was very anxious to unload the property who insisted that the reason the previous owner had left in the first place had absolutely nothing to do with the rumors that the house was infested with snakes. After a few minutes of haggling, the strategist had gotten the price for the property so low that he simply had to pull out a checkbook and write a check for the entire purchase price!

There were two incentives in this case: the taste of revenge as well as a nice piece of property for almost nothing. And, the belligerent drunk was no longer harassing the folks about the town so in the long run, everyone benefitted. This was a very good example of creative retaliation.

Then there was the ninth grade student who found himself being the subject of repeated attacks by the school bully. The bully would take lunch money, cigarettes, notebook paper, or whatever the victim happened to be carrying when he was attacked. Settling the problem in the ordinary manner was out of the question because of the difference in their sizes—the bully being considerably larger. The victim realized that if he were to survive the school year, there would have to be some changes made.

Monday morning rolled around, and the victim nervously awaited across from the school for the bell to ring, standing in his usual spot, smoking a cigarette and trying to fight off the sick feeling in the pit of his stomach. He had planned things thoroughly over the weekend, and although he knew exactly how and when his offensive would take place, he was still worried that something would go wrong. He thought about changing his mind but before he could do so, he was approached by his target.

As usual, the victim was forced, by the threat of physical violence, to relinquish whatever he had that was of value and the package of cigarettes which he was carrying in his shirt pocket. With only mild apprehension, the victim did as he was requested and listened to the bully as he laughingly remarked, "You don't need these smokes anyway! Don't you know they're bad for your health?"

The victim knew the bully's routine by heart. He would immediately retreat into the rest room with his cronies where he would spend the better part of first period sitting around cracking jokes and smoking the cigarettes they stole.

The victim followed the bully across the street and into the crowded hallway and watched him out of the corner of his eye as he disappeared into the rest room. He slowed his pace for a second or two, listening intently for the tell-tale sound that his plan had worked. Suddenly, there was a loud pop coming from the rest room, followed by screams of other students. Kids quickly filled the hallway, followed by the teachers who had been frantically summoned to the rest room by some of the others who had seen the "incident". Soon, the bully was carried out of the rest room with his face covered by a very bloody towel. The strategist smiled to himself as he walked peacefully to his class.

He learned during lunch that his target had no sooner lit a cigarette before it exploded in his face, taking off part of his lip and temporarily flash-blinding him from gunpowder and tobacco. Being told this, the strategist looked at his friend and smiled.

"Doesn't he know that smoking is bad for your health?" he asked.

In this case the strategist implanted a re-manufactured firecracker in a cigarette then placed the cigarette back in the package. The amount of powder he used was equivalent to about four of the standard Black Cat firecrackers. He had toyed with the idea of placing the projectile part of a bottle rocket in the cigarette instead, with the direction of the rocket facing the filter of the cigarette, but decided to use some technique that was capable of more destruction that a bottle rocket could wreak.

The victim's initial apprehension of the effectiveness of his planning was the result of several factors such as his own lack of belief in his own ability, the fact that he never had taken any type of physical action against anyone in the past, and concern for retaliation. Even though he made sure that his target would be carrying not only cigarettes in the package but as well a small vial of cocaine, thus the bully, once he got out of the hospital, would find himself expelled from school and possibly in juvenile detention center. The strategist knew that no-one else would smoke the loaded cigarette because it was some sort of gang code of conduct that each had to acquire his own cigarettes. It was a trait distinction that the strategist found when he was doing his planning.

Generally speaking, ingenuity can be procured from many sources including books, television, movies, hobbyist magazines, manuals such as this, as well as practical experience. Much information can also be found in public libraries, libraries at community colleges and universities, bookstores, hobby shops, and the like, but nothing beats actual, first hand experience. This applicable knowledge can be best obtained from another strategist though few are willing to share their secrets and talents for fear of legal repercussions or similar ramifications.

Yet another source of workable knowledge might come from disgruntled employees of a technical field or industry. For instance, you can pick up valuable information from an ex-phone company employee who worked as an operator, technician, lineman, installer, or almost any other capacity. He can tell you tricks of the trade with regard to tapping phone lines, special phone numbers used to access toll free telephone lines, etc. The only problem is that it is quite difficult to locate a disgruntled phone company employee who will share these secrets. If you have a friend in a position such as the above, he is a valuable friend indeed.

A chemist is yet another good source of information. For instance, he might tell you that a homemade version of napalm can be made by mixing 1 part Joy dish washing liquid to either 2 parts Benzene or 1 part gasoline. He may be able to tell you that even a more frightening form of napalm, which actually clings to whatever it comes into contact with, can be made by dissolving 2 parts polystyrene into 1 part Benzene then adding 1 part gasoline to the mixture. After carefully mixing the ingredients in their proper amounts, the resultant chemical is a very volatile form of "look alike" napalm which is about the consistency of apple jelly.

Napalm is a very strange chemical in that it supposedly can be shot around corners and clings to whatever it comes into contact with. Its incendiary properties made it a very favorable tool during WWII and Vietnam, being used by the military to spray into enemy bunkers or tunnels, to clear enemy infested brush and wooded areas, as well as many other uses.

Ingenuity, regardless from what source it came, allows a strategist a veritable armory of information which can be used when the situation necessitates the use of "out of the ordinary" tools or tricks. This information can be stored away inside a person's brain, cross referenced with other stored information, resulting in new technology or tricks for the strategist to rely upon.

One very imaginative strategist realized that he could use a jeweler's drill and a glass-cutting bit to drill tiny holes in the sealed-beam headlights of a target's automobile, inject (with a hypodermic syringe) a wide variety of chemicals into the holes including gasoline, lighter fluid, napalm (though not with the syringe), and even spray butane from cigarette lighter refill cannisters into the bulbs. Then he found that the holes should be sealed with wax, clay, gum, or something which would prevent the fumes from escaping. This being done, he would only have to wait for the target to find the need for the headlights, pull on the switch, and activate incendiary devices that would either explode, shoot flames up to twenty feet from the front of the automobile, or completely take the front fenders off of the target's vehicle.

This particular strategist also found that, by increasing or decreasing the amount of chemical he injected into the headlights, the resulting blast would be (by decreasing amounts) more of a percussion while the other extreme would result in greater incendiary display. He found, too, that he could apply the same technique to appliance bulbs in refrigerators or ranges, regular reading lamps, auto instrument panel lamps, and interior courtesy lamps. He found that just two or three drops of lighter fluid can be fatal if placed in the right device.

I cannot stress strongly enough the need for circumspection and common sense in the application of the above techniques. A single mistake, such as installing a bomb-bulb into a live circuit, can prove deadly for the attempting strategist. Only a person who is fully capable of understanding the mechanics of the system with which he is working can install such a device with any form of relative safety.

But all tricks of the trade need not be all that potentially dangerous to get a point across. This was found to be true by a plumber who found that his wife was diddling around across town while he was at work. However, prior to taking action he researched the information he had been given to be sure that it was true, knowing that rumors are seemingly a part of everyday life and should be taken with a grain of salt.

After much consideration, he decided that it was to his advantage that he not confront his wife's lover face-to-face. Himself being a meek man of about five-foot-four, his target being at least a foot taller and at least a hundred pounds heavier. Instead, he decided to make his act of aggression a bit more suited to his line of expertise.

He waited for his target to busy himself away from home then slowed his panel van to a stop in front of the target's home. Before he drove into his target's neighborhood, however, he had placed magnetic signs over his own advertising on the van to disguise it as belonging to a water testing company.

He removed a Freon gas cannister from the back of the van which had been filled with compressed air (although Freon would have done more damage) and nonchalantly carried the cannister across the yard and connected it to the target's garden water spigot via a hose he had made for the occasion. He opened the water valve, then the cannister valve, effectively dumping over a hundred p.s.i. of compressed air into the water lines of the house. The can emptied, he closed off both valves then returned to the truck and drove away.

Commonly, a household plumbing system and the things attached to it are not capable of withstanding such a high pressure. This is very true of the valves and lines within a toilet tank. Pressure such as this can easily blow shower heads off their fixtures, explode the mechanism inside automatic ice-makers in new freezers, and completely devastate faucets and toilet controls. If the pressure is great enough, it can also cause a porcelain toilet to explode into thousands of pieces as soon as the handle on the tank is depressed.

Imagine, if you will, an unsuspecting victim sitting on the toilet as he twists the handle to flush it. It would not be out of the ordinary course of events for the victim to find himself no longer sitting on the toilet but in a puddle of surprise!

Personally, this isn't exactly what I would call poetic revenge, but a person has his own tolerance of things and tends to evaluate circumstances differently from others.

There are as many devices and improvised items as there are people who use them. Some are to be found around the home or shop while others can be rather expensive, and still others can be not only expensive but even the acquisition can be a dangerous undertaking. On the lesser extreme, there exists a little piece of electronic gadgetry which is very small, very cheap, and will drive a person bananas! This is a little device which emits a very loud, high pitched chirp that can be preset for specific time intervals or set to sound at random intervals. Although this device may not sound very useful, don't be fooled! Imagine sitting in a quiet office or even a library when suddenly a cricket starts chirping. When trying to focus upon a particular task, this sound can be very distracting and when you begin to search for the culprit, it can't be located. The random interval chirps are too high pitched for our ears to "fix" on, the sound bounces off tables, walls, desks, etc, and cannot be pin pointed. You may attempt to go on about your business but soon find that the more you try to concentrate the less you get accomplished because the incessant chirping keeps redirecting your attention!

Another simple and inexpensive device is an "on/off" delay timer which can be connected in an electrical circuit to either switch the circuit on or off at a preset time. Consider a person flying a private plane, for instance, as he realizes that his auto-pilot has engaged and the plane cannot be released from its path of projection. Then, as suddenly as the auto-pilot engaged, it disengages, relinquishing control to the pilot. These timers can be set for several seconds or several minutes, and in either case the pilot finds it immediately necessary to set the plane down to get it checked as well as to clean out his trousers!

Such switches can be placed on automobile electrical systems, boats, motorcycles, or on the overhead light bar of emergency vehicles. The overall purpose can be to invoke unparalleled fear or to just let the target know that he is vulnerable.

Such has been an overview of the physical approach, let's move on to the Emotional Approach.

EMOTIONAL APPROACH

It may not seem like it, but there is a definite delineation between the emotional and the mental approaches. The difference is the fact that the emotional key incorporates a more psychological methodology to the extent of playing on phobias and fears exclusively as the Achille's heel of the target. This technique is sometimes more difficult to employ and usually affords better results for the more professional or experienced strategist, but used successfully can leave emotional scars on the target for years to come, perhaps even for a lifetime. The strategist must be able to identify the psychological or emotional problem area, isolate it from other idiosyncrasies, then exploit it for its value.

For instance, a person exhibiting a paranoia complex can be pushed over the edge by having their paranoia fed until the fears are no longer imagined but are acted upon as valid considerations. If a strategist finds that a target has a paranoid complex, he may play on this with acts such as leaving a blank sheet of paper slid beneath the target's front door, leaving the target to write his own (although mental) message. To a normal mind, this may not seem too very devastating but it IS! Even though the message was written in the mind of the target, it would be ten-fold more effective than to put tangible words on the paper for the target to attempt to rationalize. The strategist can never fully know the motivational factors which are instilled within the mental processes of his target, and the target will always assume the meaning of the blank sheet of paper as being directed towards that which lies at the base of his fears.

The above technique works even better if the strategist can manage to leave a sheet of paper which happens to be the target's favorite color, or perhaps has the target's letterhead affixed. It should remain as a precautionary word that the strategist should never underestimate the professional connections of the target and therefor be sure not to leave a speedy return address upon the paper which are known as fingerprints!

Another simple technique which can be used with the above is to find out what (if any) kind of cigarettes the target smokes, or what kind of gum he chews, his favorite cologne, or some personal item such as this. On the day the paper is slid under the door, leave a personal item (cigarettes, candy, etc.) in a place accessible only to the target. Add a few late night "wrong number" phone calls, calling his work number with a very urgent message but hanging up the phone before he answers, are things which quickly excite the target's imagination into believing there are many people lurking in the darkness waiting to pounce upon him as he sleeps. Eventually, every sound in the night and everything which is even remotely out of the ordinary can push him closer to the point of no return.

The line of delineation between the mental and the emotional approaches lies in whether or not the target structures his life around his fears or weaknesses.

Under the Freudian school of thought, man is driven by three motivational factors: sex, fear, and aggression. These factors are said to be instinctive and ultimately create the mechanism which allows us to survive and procreate our species. Accordingly, any disturbance or interference with these factors (especially during childhood) will cause an emotional scar upon an individual's psyche which he will carry for the remainder of his life. By the discovery of this emotional scar, a strategist can quite effectively manipulate his target through a wide variety of techniques even to the extent of totally brainwashing the target.

If a person is rewarded for an expressed behavior then

it is quite likely that that particular behavior will be continued to be expressed and strengthened through the system of rewards. If the behavior is punished, however, then it will diminish over a period of time. The strict and determinate key is that in order for the strategist to manipulate the behavior, he has to do his homework to find out what it is that the target would view as punishment and what he would perceive as reward.

By the same methodology, a strategist could step up to a handicapped person and kick away a crutch, replace it with something better suited to the handicapped person, and the strategist would quickly be viewed as good or helpful. If the replacement crutch is one which can be easily manipulated by the strategist, so much the better.

The two most elusive and studied emotions within the realm of psychology are fear and anxiety. These are, consequently, the self-same elements which the strategist attempts to focus upon in the mental and emotional approaches of offensive strategy. It has been learned that fear has an identifiable cause where anxiety does not, which simply means that fear is the descriptive emotion of a person's reaction to a situation which is frightening or unfamiliar. Anxiety on the other hand is the emotion which is felt upon the realization that a person has no control over an inescapable or unavoidable situation to which the outcome is unknown. For instance, a person who commits a crime may fear the police (with cause) but will experience anxiety once he is apprehended due to the fact that he is no longer in control of the situation; the control now being in someone else's hands which will invariably cause punishment to be inflicted upon him.

To summarize, there are three approaches which the

strategist should know and understand: mental, physical, and emotional. Each of these can be successfully employed by a strategist only if he fully and completely examines in its entirety the situation at hand through a method which is known as situational analysis. In this analysis, the strategist attempts to locate and isolate any one of the many weak spots which is inherent of the target due to the fact that a common condition shared by all human beings is imperfection. The strategist needs to know his own strengths and weaknesses, those of his target, then there needs to be a comparison to see in which areas the target is most vulnerable to the respective strategist.

As I mentioned above, human beings are creatures of imperfection and because of this it stands to reason that the products and procreations of this species are likewise imperfect. It is quite impossible for an imperfect species to create, appreciate, or even fully realize the true conception of perfection. Philosophically, we can only imagine a rationalized concept of perfection but only to the extent of it being relative to the particular state of being in which we exist. Due to this property of imperfection, we have to realize that every person has a particular weakness which expresses his imperfection. Once it has been found, the strategist can gain full control over his target by merely manipulating the weakness through external influence. It is somewhat of an axiom, to interject, that anything made-made can be man-destroyed.

A point must be made clear: a person must rely upon his own resources and intellectual abilities, prowess, and imagination, and be prepared at once to improvise because many situations will undoubtedly require improvisational techniques in order to custom tailor an offensive assault and bring it about to a satisfactory or optimum conclusion. And there must be a conclusion to the offensive so it won't be left hanging. Sometimes when we bring in our wash from the clothes lines, we find that our clothes get dirtier after they've been hung out to dry for a spell. A strategist would do well, then, to update and upgrade his craft while constantly and continually keeping an open mind and a flexible perspective which will enhance his chances for survival.

3

Tools and Toys

It has been said that you can tell the difference between men and boys by the price of their toys. In this case, however, the difference lies not in the price of the toys in-as-much as it lies within the type of the toy. While there are literally thousands of so-called prefabricated toys which would work well in many retaliatory offenses, situations generally require on-site preparation and the use of materials which are simply at hand. (Ever watch *MacGyver* on television?) Besides, the most effective devices are the ones which are the simplest and can be built with materials found around the home or shop. In almost every instance, the strategist should learn to be self-sufficient and improvisational with respect to his immediate necessities and surroundings. He should bear in mind, however, that if a particular device requires special ingredients, it wouldn't necessarily be wise to leave a name and a phone number if the ingredients have to be special ordered.

With this in mind, I have illustrated a few of the simpler devices which, as you can see, are constructed out of quite ordinary stuff which can be found in almost any store, including the corner Stop and Shop (otherwise known as the Stop and Rob).

Again, there are literally hundreds of thousands of devices which can and have been constructed for use in certain situations, and there would not be ample space within this book to attempt to illustrate them all. With this in mind, I have decided to exemplify only a few of them over the following pages; ones which will at least open the mind of the strategist to sort of tickle his imagination.

Simple Time Delay Device

This is one of the simplest of all devices to construct. As shown, all that are needed are a book of "Gopher" matches and a cigarette. This device has been known to effectively ignite anything which requires heat or flame for ignition.

As you see, the filter of the cigarette should be positioned in such a manner that it is hidden behind the matchheads so that when the cover of the book is closed, and the cigarette burns down, the cigarette ember will ignite the first match and result in a chain reaction

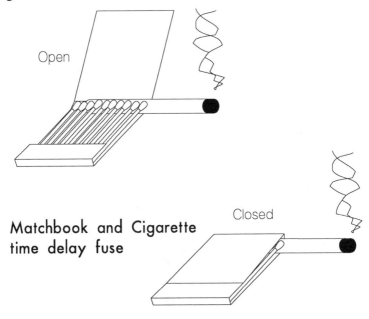

Open

Matchbook and Cigarette
time delay fuse

Closed

whereby all of the matches are ignited spontaneously.

The book of matches, with the cigarette in place, can be stood on its side in or within close proximity to almost any volatile chemical. The cigarette should be such that it is pointed upwards. Again, the length of the cigarette determines the actual time delay of the device and usually runs from five to twelve minutes.

As the strategist will learn, health hazards from cigarettes do not always come from smoking them!

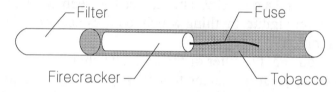

Booby-Trapped Cigarette

Booby Trapped Cigarette

Illustration 2 is pretty much self explanatory but a couple of points should be stressed. First, care should be taken when refilling the tobacco around the cigarette due to the fact that a fresh cigarette is tightly packed. Also, if the tobacco is loose, it will not burn properly and will perhaps alert the target to the fact that something may be wrong (this is especially true if the target happens to be naturally over-paranoid.)

To avoid this, the strategist should take care in preparing the device (as in all devices) and not be in a hurry.

There are many variations of this device which are as easily constructed as the one illustrated above. One of the variations being the implantation of a bottle rocket instead of a firecracker. The direction of travel can either be away from or towards the target, depending upon the effects which the strategist desires.

Timed Delayed Incendiary Device

The device depicted in figure 3 illustrates another time delay device which requires the use of a few firecrackers (or bottle rocket), a pinch of sealing wax, and a plastic cannister of cigarette lighter fluid. The construction is very simple. It should also be noted that the more fluid there is in the bottle, the greater incendiary effect.

It should also be interjected that this is a very dangerous and volatile device and misuse can cause permanent disfigurement, blindness, or even death! Common sense should dictate that any device or similarly fashioned device could easily be met with the same conclusion. BEWARE!

When the folks at the lighter fluid companies began producing their products in the plastic cannisters, they created a Pandora's box of explosive possibilities. The containers are perfect for storing, transporting, and provide quick and easy assembly of many innovative devices. Warning! Do not toss these cannisters into a microwave oven! They will explode almost immediately and result in a somewhat radioactive fireball!

Time Delayed Incendiary Device for Automobile

The device in figure 4 also makes use of a plastic cannister of cigarette lighter fluid but can be connected to an automobile electrical system. There are no special tools required and all of the ingredients can be found in any shop or garage. Properly installed, the device can be devastating to any vehicle.

The tools needed for proper installation are a 5 inch length of clothes hanger wire, approximately 3 feet of shielded electrical wire with alligator clips attached to both ends, a 3 inch long wood screw (small diameter),

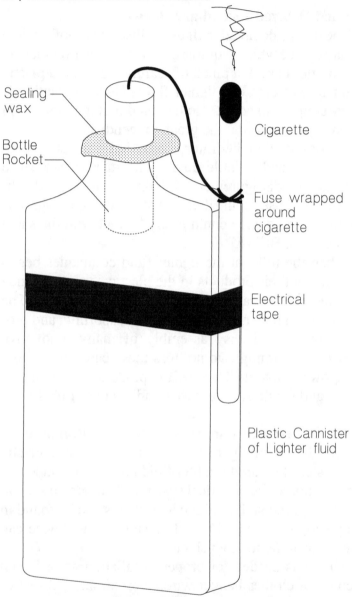

Sealing wax

Bottle Rocket

Cigarette

Fuse wrapped around cigarette

Electrical tape

Plastic Cannister of Lighter fluid

Time Delayed Incendiary Device

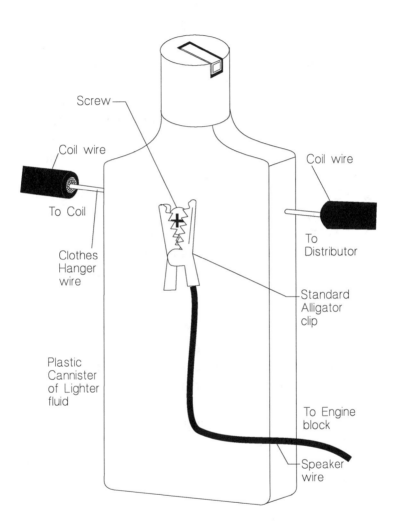

Time Delayed Incendiary Device For Automobile or Vehicle Installation

a pocket knife and a plastic cannister of fluid.

As in the illustration, the sides of the cannister need to be punctured and the wire inserted through the cannister so that there is an even protrusion on either side. The wood screw should be implanted in the front of the cannister in such a manner that it is about an eighth of an inch away from the wire on the inside of the cannister. At this point, the coil wire of the target's automobile should be cut in half and threaded onto the clothes hanger wire (see illustration.) The 3 foot length of wire should now be clipped to the wood screw on one end and the other end clipped to the frame or engine block of the car in order to ground the device.

If it has been properly installed, when the ignition of the car is hot, a spark will jump from the clothes hanger to the wood screw, igniting the contents of the cannister.

Improvised Device to Pressurize Plumbing

The device in illustration 5 is pretty much self explanatory as well. To use, the water hydrant reducer fitting must be installed on the air hose and clamped tightly in place. Once in place, the fitting can be attached to an outside faucet of the target's house, the water valve opened widely, then the air release valve opened on the Freon cannister. This will allow the air in the cannister to escape into the target's water lines, such lines not being made to handle the increased pressure. After the cannister is depleted of contents, the water faucet should be quickly closed, followed by the valve on the cannister.

Once the target opens any water valve in his house, the water will force through it with a dangerous pressure expulsion. This expulsion has been known to blast

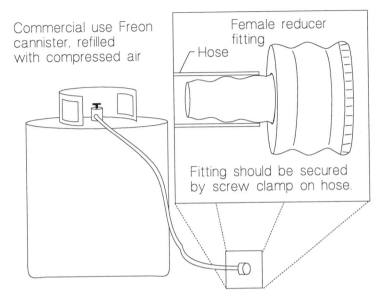

Commercial use Freon cannister, refilled with compressed air

Female reducer fitting

Hose

Fitting should be secured by screw clamp on hose.

shower heads off the wall, blow the auto-fill mechanism out of hot water heaters, and have been reported to have blown urinals from the walls of others.

Also, instead of using compressed air in the lines, an alternative is to use Freon (which will freeze the water and burst the lines) or to use Butane or natural gas. The latter is extremely dangerous and should be used only as a last alternative. If the escaping gas is met with the spark from a cigarette as it escapes, it will cause a very devastating explosion. BE WARNED.

Also, it is a felony in most states to possess the Freon cannisters once the original contents have been depleted. It is likewise a felony to refill them or to transport them for ANY purpose. This tidbit of information IS worth being aware of!

These aren't the only devices which can be manufactured for improvisational use. By far, they are exceeded by the imagination of each individual strategist and by the availability of intelligence and gadgets already in the market place. One can construct a quickie bomb by wrapping a Butane (disposable) lighter in tape and firecrackers.

Whatever the device, the primary concern is for the safety of the user. Note that all devices contained herein ARE FOR ENTERTAINMENT PURPOSES ONLY.

The following devices are self explanatory, and have been discussed in an earlier section.

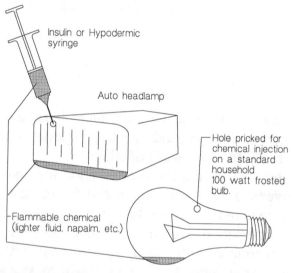

Insulin or Hypodermic syringe

Auto headlamp

Hole pricked for chemical injection on a standard household 100 watt frosted bulb.

Flammable chemical (lighter fluid, napalm, etc.)

Bulb Explosive Devices
Once the chemical has been injected, the hole should be plugged to prevent spilling of the chemical.

Mousetrap Circuit Switch
This is a very useful device in any situation which requires personnel activation of a detonating device. It is very simply constructed of the materials shown in the

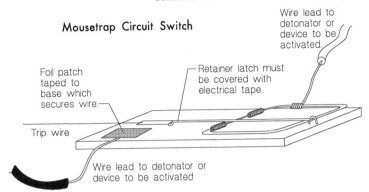

Mousetrap Circuit Switch

Wire lead to detonator or device to be activated.

Foil patch taped to base which secures wire.

Retainer latch must be covered with electrical tape.

Trip wire

Wire lead to detonator or device to be activated

illustration and is fool-proof. In the construction of the device, however, the retainer latch MUST be completely covered with electrical tape. Otherwise, once the device is set, the current between the lead wires will short through the retainer latch thus completing the circuit prematurely.

A string is attached to the trip-latch which is then stretched across a pathway and secured to a stationary object. The wire leads are connected to the detonator or device as shown in the illustration after the spring-jaw is properly secured.

There are several points to consider BEFORE attempting to use this device. First, it has a hair-trigger and any sudden movement or vibration of the device can cause it to spring shut. Therefore, it should be armed in the following manner:

1) The device should be located and secured in place by tape, string, etc.

2) The trip-cord should then be strung to its destination and securely attached.

3) The spring-jaw should be set and the device should be lightly tapped to make sure that it will not prematurely snap shut.

4) At this point, the lead wires can be connected to their destination, whether it be a buzzer, detonator, or other device.

If there is any variation in the arming of this device , the result will be a premature ignition of whatever device this switch controls. Depending upon the nature of the main device, the result could range from embarrassment to, well, you get the idea.

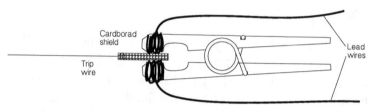

Clothes Pin Device.

A variation to the device above is a very simple item which incorporates a clothes pin, two lead wires, electrical tape, a length of string, and a piece of card board. It is rigged in much the same manner as the mousetrap, but there is no spring latching mechanism.

The lead wires should be stripped and wrapped around the jaws of the clothes pin. The clothes pin should be located and secured in place with tape. The piece of cardboard, after attaching the length of string, should be clamped between the jaws thus separating the shielding the lead wires from each other. The other end of the string should be strung either across a walkway or attached to a doorknob. The lead wires can now be connected to the primary device.

The operation is simple. When the cardboard is removed from the jaws, the wire ends are allowed to touch each other and the circuit is then completed.

4

Blackmail Theory

In this chapter we'll examine the psychological foundations of blackmail towards practical applications, and there is a reason for this approach. Of all the manipulative techniques used by man for the control of others, blackmail is one of the oldest and most successful ever utilized. This technique can bring even a paragon of virtue to his knees and make him beg and whimper like a scolded puppy. It can destroy love, break homes, seed hatred, and even effectively cripple governments by focusing upon key officials. When used correctly, it can be a dangerous and insidious curse which, once administered, can be everlasting and even passed from one family generation to the next, thus debilitating the target's heirs. And no person is immune from this device. By action, it has been likened to quicksand in that it holds a victim within its clutches and slowly sucks the victim beneath the surface of the mire even unto the throes of death!

Blackmail, as defined by Webster, is the extortion of a person by the means of intimidation. The exact origin of blackmail has been lost to the annals of history. However, it has been dated as far back as the Socraterian era and has been in active use ever since.

Intimidation is the operative word in the definition because this is what gives blackmail its fangs. But what is intimidation? What principles allow it to work? There is no exact answer except that as stated throughout this book, that every person has a weakness or an imperfection which is a key element to his motivational instinct. There are no exceptions to this rule. A person's ego, personality, social standing, greed, and even the basic survival motive are all determining factors of how much value a person places upon this weakness, and how important it is for him to keep it from the view of anyone else.

His value of importance in combination with the value which a person places upon his own existence, as well as his concern for others and the depth of his altruistic instincts, are all variables which allow intimidation to operate.

Weak spots can be viewed in differing terms but what it basically means is that there are skeletons in the closets. They can have such for a basis as embarrassment, illegal or illicit events which would invariably cause the loss of social standing and respect, or even the loss of personal freedom.

Psychologically, the primary catalysts are fear, pain, and anxiety. Secondarily, threats of pain, social deprivation, the removal or deprivation of essential necessities, the threat to personal safety, and the threat of the unknown which is the origin of anxiety. The catalyst in any case can be one or a combination of any or all of these factors, or others which are too many to attempt to discuss at this time. Before any of these can be effectively utilized, though, we must still understand why they are able to work.

Intimidation is loosely referred to as that which instills within a person various negative feelings of fear and emotion or the absence of a feeling of well-being, such is the loss of security. Although the exact concept of fear is still not fully understood, we do know however, that the anticipation of a negative event is what actually inflicts the initial damage. For example, if a person gets shot in the head and never realized that the threat of death was upon him, he would not have had the motivation to make necessary adjustments in his behavior patterns so that the threat may not have existed in the first place. (Ducking or getting the hell out of the way.) On the other hand, if he had some sense of forewarning, his attitude would have been one of fear and apprehension but not of getting shot in-as-much as the fear of the unknown or the anxiety of having little or no control over the situation.

So, the base of all anxiety is fear. Either fear which is real such as an immediate and recognizable threat, or the fear that is imagined and irrational such as exhibited in phobias. Although one is real and the other is imagined, they both create the same state of anxiety which is physically manifested.

Anxiety can cause physiological changes within a person which collectively are referred to as the "fight or flight" syndrome. In the mind, when a person faces a threatening situation his reaction is to either flee from the element of danger, retreat to a place of relative safety, or to remain and face the consequences of his actions. In either case, the brain begins to prepare the body for what is to come. As these physiological changes begin to take place several things begin to happen in quick succession which are known as the "general adaptation syndrome." (G.A.S.) These occurrences are described as follows.

Our physiological make-up is such that our bodies

react in the same manner whether the threat is real or if it is imagined. As a real source, it can be from such things as injury, illness, or disease. From an imagined source a perceived threat might be seen in a rapidly mushrooming argument or a strong feeling (without reason) of an impending life-threatening illness or accident.

The body first begins to prepare for the fight by increased heart rate, respiration, and drastically increased blood-sugar content, otherwise known as an adrenaline rush. Once these systems have been activated and fully mobilized, they remain in this alert stage until the threat has passed or until the body has reached a state of exhaustion. If exhaustion is due to a prolonged state of physical stress, or if the body isn't re-nourished and rested, the result could be death. Psychological stress rarely causes death but can severely interrupt or disrupt other bodily functions.

Knowing this and being able to make more accurate generalizations of human behavior from cross sampling or estimation, we can predict (to some extent) how much a person will allow himself to be exposed to before taking some sort of corrective action. This is called the reaction threshold and, although it is an accurate generalization of averaged data, it is still unique of each individual alive.

It is interesting to know that what one person perceives as fear, another may perceive as mere entertainment or as a magnet, drawing him into its midst. Each persons' concept of fear and the resulting experiences are unique to each individual. The focus then must be on the target's points of vulnerability which activate his system of fear: fear of damage to the ego, pride, self esteem, or physical damage or pain. Secondarily are the mechanisms which afford protection.

The weakest spot within an individual will generally lie within his life-style which subconsciously exhibits and exploits his personality. If the target is a business professional or the executive type, a devout family man, P.T.A. and the Wednesday afternoon Bridge club, the weak spot will be the common denominator of all the activities which make up his life-style per se, his personality, in this case his status as a family oriented, structured person. Efforts in this case should be directed in locating a substantial piece of information which, if exploited, would be a direct threat to his state of social existence or his life-style. Essentially, one or more of the three basic necessities for survival must be threatened: food, clothing, or shelter.

In the planning stage of the offensive, the strategist must make what I call the potential damage assessment. This is where he actually evaluates a potential weak spot (whether it be personal or sexual habits, the use of illegal substances either by the target or a closely associated person, etc.) This is much like the planning of war by playing war-games on a computer and assessing the outcome from any of the variables or moves that can be made. In our case, the assessment would be made by looking at the weak spot in relation to the target's life-style, associations, or even the target's mental or physical stability if the weakness is exploited, and to what extent the weakness would have to be exploited in order to achieve optimum results. The strategist then rates the existence of secondary damage in terms of others who may also be exposed to the threat, or the fall-out factor. He should keep in mind that if more than one person could potentially suffer from such an exploitation, the value of the weakness my sharply increase but the success potential will invariably decrease in respect. Also, with the added number of targets within a particular evaluation or assessment, there is also an increased risk of danger to the strategist from unforeseen retaliatory efforts.

In general terms, blackmail threatens the exposure of something which a person would rather, for one reason or another, keep confidential. However, for blackmail to be effective, the strategist's plan must be able to be brought to a point of conclusion. For instance, if a target has a weak spot, and the strategist's planning is thorough, yet for some reason the target finds that he really has nothing to lose by calling the strategist into the open with the threat, the plan obviously will not work. Likewise, if the strategist has made one or more miscalculations about the importance or value of the weakness to the target, the plan still may not be able to follow through and in fact may turn on the strategist and placing a new threat in the game but this one in the strategist's court.

And, since blackmail is a crime in itself, the threat must be made in such a way as not to expose the strategist or his accomplices (and I use this as an example, because I, personally, would NEVER rely upon the help of someone else in any such endeavor due to the fact that one witness to an event is the one that will then have something on me.) It should also be noted that when there no longer exists a real threat to the target, the entire operation should be dismantled and quickly disposed of. Never attempt to bluff in a situation such as I just mentioned, either. That would be analogous to holding an unloaded gun on a Grizzly bear!

It should be known that some people and organizations have immunity from prosecution of their involvement in a crime or similar situation due to their past or current political affiliations, diplomatic status, etc. The target of such an attempt may be able to quickly turn the table on the strategist and turning witness for the state against others who may be implicated in the weakness. It is therefore extremely advantageous for the strategist to know all of the contingencies and ramifications of his actions current or pending, as well as all of the factors surrounding the potential weakness which he seeks to exploit. Blackmail isn't a congenial game of poker. If there is indeed a bluff and if it is called, the stakes generally aren't definable in monetary terms.

5

Information Procurement and Analysis

The topic of this chapter is the finding of various types of information and the assessment of same with respect to possible application by the strategist. Information can be used for many purposes and likewise be obtained, gleaned, or gathered from a wide array of sources, both legal and slightly "less than legal."

Information is most readily available from the basic standpoint of the physical search by the strategist. This usually involves foot work, determination, patience, a keen ear, as well as the ability to interpret useful information and that which is not readily useful to be stored for future reference. Also, the strategist must have (or develop) the ability to discern truth from the course of a normal conversation between himself and strangers whom he has no knowledge of their honesty or lack thereof.

The physical search for information must always be a basic starting point. The search begins with the locating and assessment of leads. These are tidbits of information and facts with which a strategist begins the piecing of a puzzle. They are found to be instructive in many respects, in that they may direct a strategist to bigger chunks of information. They may give only hints as to other relative information. They can provide names, dates, locations, subject identification, and statistical information. Leads are most commonly cross-referenced with other leads, analyzed for possibilities, and filed according to their potential worth. Once a lead has been filed, however, it becomes idle information. And leads won't usually jump up and shout "Here I am! Come and get me!" In order to find them you generally have to actively search for them. I am reminded of a man who was searching diligently for a specific piece of information when someone asked him what it was that he was searching for. He smiled and replied, "When I find it then I'll know." Such is the case with leads.

The location of potential sources of information vary depending upon the target, but most usually can be found in the form of the target's friends, enemies, business acquaintances, neighbors, hair stylist, or can be found in the form of gossip which floats freely around country clubs, social gatherings, and even church. Incidentally, if the enemies can be identified and located, especially if they are former friends or business associates, they can provide much useful information pertaining to the target. It has been said that a lot can be told about a person by the company he keeps, and this includes both good and bad relationships. Another interesting point to remember is that friends will lie for friends as will enemies will lie against their enemies! The strategist must be tactful, however, and must learn to extract information from either casual conversation or conversation which he actually "directs" for the sole purpose of obtaining information. However, he must not appear too greedy nor should he dwell too long on a particular aspect of his curiosity else he is liable to tip his hand. He must learn to be subtle and to take whatever he can get and make the most of it.

Information can be found in the form of public records such as those found in the county or district clerks' offices: divorce recordings, marriage decrees, birth/death certificates, new businesses, etc. Still other information can be found in the records of credit reporting agencies, employment personnel offices, and general character references which the strategist can solicit by telephone. It would behoove the would-be strategist to spend a few hours at a public or a university library and study the subject of investigative technique. He will find the information to be quite rewarding and useful.

As the information is acquired, it should be laid out like a jigsaw puzzle and all of the pieces should be then compared for association or fit against each other. In this manner a general picture will begin to appear and the strategist will soon be able to focus upon one aspect of the entire puzzle with a narrower focus in mind. Soon the strategist will learn to presuppose or even predict future pieces of the puzzle, then be able to direct his efforts towards a precise flaw within the target's character or personal realm of existence.

This method is a very basic approach which relies upon the strategist's prowess and intellect, as well as the possible permutations, combinations, and outcome probability relating to the pieces of the puzzle. If the outcome can be predicted before the puzzle has been completed then the pieces are nothing more than a formality which is necessary for checking data for accuracy or gaining physical evidence for whatever purposes desired.

The next technique is somewhat more interesting and makes use of information which has been obtained from isolated sources of physical locales such as a target's home, office, or other location where the target has a specific interest. Generally, this form of information is that which can be procured by means of listening devices, room bugs, or voice retrieval systems such as in use by the federal government for similar reasons. I must say that in-as-much as these systems are effective, so are they generally illegal except with relative exception. Again, it wouldn't hurt for the strategist to do a little homework and check on the current related legal code in his area to know the legal ramifications of gathering information through electronic sources. The one major exception which I am instantly aware of is the use of a parabolic microphone, or the gathering of information which is commonly available in the form of radio transmission.

These exceptions are legal because of a supreme court ruling which essentially states that anything which can be pulled out of the airwaves (radio wave included) without the implanting of special equipment without the knowledge and express permission of the person who is the subject of the information gathering efforts, is commonly within the public domain. This ruling was primarily directed towards the satellite television industry but is relatively unspecific. In short, whatever a person has the capabilities of extracting from the airwaves through whatever capabilities and equipment he may have is fair game. However, there is an exception here as well which pertains to information which originates from law enforcement or similar agencies, or from agencies within the federal government: It should be stressed that a strategist should never reveal the content of any information he may overhear coming from these sources, and should contact the FCC for legal updates which are related to this subject. Again, it never hurts for a strategist to be wise to the ways and means of the legal world if he can do so without being caught up in the legal system from the receiving end! Those are the negative aspects.

The positive aspects are that for the general information purposes which pertains to almost all of the information which is available from monitoring electronics transmissions are in public domain or at least a person who is monitoring such transmission cannot be traced in 99.9% of the times. The information he receives, if he keeps it confidential, is most-times extremely informative and even priceless to the strategist. As a matter of fact, I urge anyone who wishes to monitor radio communications to have a pen and a notebook handy when doing so, due to the information which can be overheard. If the strategist can afford one, I would go so far as to suggest connecting a tape recorder to the monitoring device so that all conversation can be kept intact for "posterity".

To illustrate the effectiveness of this type of system, I will relate to one law enforcement agency which regularly monitors radio transmissions to gain information relating to prostitution, drug movement, and other illegal activities. They usually get vast amounts of information regarding names, dates, locations, and other data then just happen to appear at a vantage point to actually witness an illegal transaction. If a particular bust gets to court the officers state that they obtained their information through the process of "discovery" or that the information was simply "overheard" and acted upon. Thus the officers do not admit to possible illegal activity, civil rights of all involved remain intact, and the officers then continue to use their "process of discovery" until their sources of information run dry. Many times over this system is allowed to continue due to several facts, the least of which would be that there is essentially no illegal activity involved. Also, the time and money which would be spent on an investigation to determine the legality of their actions would be effortless due to the fact that radio monitoring equipment cannot be traced or monitored.

Also, I have heard it through the grapevine that there are other folks who use this same system to get the same information on illegal activity. In one county, a small group of people use this system to learn the times, dates, and locations of drug movements, then appear at the location and seize the drugs as well as the money from those involved. Their system works due to the fact that they are well armed, trained, and prepared for almost any contingency. Besides, who's going to call the police and report the theft of drugs or the cash with which such drugs were to be purchased?

Some of the more legitimate forms of accessing communications comes in the form of what is called a hand held, programmable, multi-band police scanner, but don't let the name fool you! This little gadget accesses much more than just police communications! The investment for a top of the line model usually runs in the neighborhood of $400.00 but the investment is well worth the expense. Accessories such as an external antenna (multi band), an ac/dc power supply, a good set of ni-cad batteries, an ear-phone, and a radio frequency manual will cost an extra $75.00, but I would urge the investment be made.

The frequency manual, otherwise known as a scan guide or frequency directory, is very similar to a telephone directory except that instead of phone numbers, the frequency directory features the particular radio frequencies for specific companies or agencies. The information is referenced by the headings of city, county, state, and federal agencies, private companies or corporations (such as television stations, security companies, armored car companies, etc.), and the information is cross referenced by frequencies, agency name, state, city, etc. Also included in such directories are frequencies by allocation (the allotted space which a certain industry is given by the Federal Communications Commission) which includes new or out-of-date allocations as well. There are several agencies which prepare these directories but I have found that the most complete and up to date issues can be found floating around scanning or monitoring clubs and even some retail outlets (such as the one where the scanner was purchased). One such manual which I am aware of includes information on such agencies as the CIA, the FBI, the IRS, and other such interesting agencies.

So, what good does this information do you? Plenty! There are literally hundreds of forms of communications which can be monitored and heretofore thought of as private communications. Devices such as mobile telephones, voice pagers, cordless telephones, wireless intercoms, remote microphones (such as the news reporters wear for the television on the spot newscast), and communications such as used for emergency services, police department low power surveillance equipment, and a myriad of other devices. All of these devices can be monitored from a distance of several blocks to several miles. On the average, however, the two-way equipment I once used could be monitored for about the distance of a mile and a half.

Particularly, the frequencies for most cordless phones, low power police surveillance devices, and personnel communicators generally lies within the 49.0 through 50.0 Mhz, as does most room bugs and wireless microphones.

Mobile, or cellular telephones are a very interesting source of listening pleasure, but the frequencies for these change quickly so it would be wise to consult your local radio dealer to find out specific allocations, or the frequencies can be found in the frequency directory I mentioned earlier. I will add that there are two types of carrier services: radio common carrier (RCC) and good old Ma Bell. You will undoubtedly find that other carriers can be found throughout the country.

To exemplify the type of information which can be accessed from a mobile telephone, a Sheriff in a southern state (a few years ago) happened to overhear drug dealers making a connection. The Sheriff was monitoring with a hand-held scanner and the dealers were talking on mobile phones. He listened intently and within a short time had enough evidence to uphold an arrest even though the communications existed between mobile phones and private residential services.

Of course, other communications pertain to much more mundane things such as stock market transactions, real estate speculation, and high priced call-girl, escort, and prostitution services. Then there is the operator assisted phone calls (in over 70% of the time) where the operator is given a phone number as well as a calling card or credit card number for billing purposes. Of course, that's just stuff you'll have to overlook because it's unlawful to use another person's account numbers! These scanners can also be used to pick up information from the aviation band such as aircraft communications of all major and private airlines, and occasionally a "near-miss" or even an in-flight emergency or accident can be heard. Scanners can be used to listen to ham radio operators, fire, medical, police, fire, armored car services, search and rescue operations, NASA, taxi-cab services, and weather updates, as well as the hundreds of other agencies for which there isn't enough space to list here.

An interjection: the type and brand of scanner purchased makes a considerable determination as to what type of communications can be monitored. It is quite possible to monitor all of the above systems on a single scanner, but a strategist must purchase a multi-band receiver to do so. This scanner should be portable (although others are available, for the strategist's use the unit should be very portable), keypad controlled, and cover the ranges of 30 to 50 (or 54 Mhz), 108-132 Mhz, 138-174 Mhz, the UHF low, high, government "T" band, and the 800 "giga" bands. The local electronics or hobbyist store can help to locate this type of scanner and almost always have them in stock.

But back to a scanner's potential. There are a wide variety of listening devices on the market, most of which can be monitored for a Walkman, or even the standard FM car stereo and from distances of up to 1/2 mile or better. But to get the best reception and the most secure form of accessing available, a strategist will have to purchase a more expensive listening device as well as a corresponding monitor, a scanner can be used in lieu of the monitor.

Some of the bugging devices are called spikes, which are simply driven like nail through the outer wall of a house or a building and which contains an internal, hidden microphone and transmitter. There are also wireless mics and room bugs which can be purchased from the hobby shop or more expensive ones can be purchased through mail order supply stores. There is also a very sensitive device called a window mic which attaches to a window via a suction cup then uses the glass to act as a sound wave gatherer, picking up all conversation within a room. I have had the experience of using a very sophisticated version of the window mic which was called a laser mic.

The laser mic is a small, hand-held laser gun which is aimed at a window from an automobile. The window can be of another car, a business establishment, office building (several floors up), or a private residence. The laser beam hits the glass in pulses many times faster than the vibration caused on the glass by the human voice. The beam is bounced off the glass and back to the transmitter where the pulses are read and digitally recreated in the form of human voice.

The strategist must then decide for himself which type or types of equipment are best suited for his needs and purchase accordingly. He must look at variables such as expense, use, legality, and convenience of installation of equipment in order to make an accurate decision. Also, he must look for the outlets by which these devices can be purchased and must be able to get around certain restrictions in the purchase of this equipment. All obstacles surpassed, once the device is in place it will spew forth information for as long as the batteries hold out (unless the device is connected to a constant power source) or until the device is discovered (God forbid).

One last reminder: It is unlawful to divulge any information heard while monitoring or to make use of such information for one's personal gain or benefit, so beware!

6

Applied Theory

Ever since Charles Bronson portrayed the vigilante on the *Death Wish* movies, many stories have begun to surface pertaining to actual accounts of vigilantism and seeking revenge. However, only a small percent of those that have actually taken place ever reach the news media for fear of enticing others to follow suit. Those that do actually make it to the eyes of the public on television programs such as *Geraldo* are used only as cases to exploit the feelings and emotions of those involved in particular instances and to increase the respective program's viewer ratings and audience numbers. It equates to increased dollars for the broadcast companies and television stations. One piece of statistical information not usually brought to the surface for public scrutiny are the statistical decreases in crime in geographical locations where vigilantism has been reported. It has been said that this is due to "professional jealousy" of the justice system due to the fact that someone besides they can actually make a difference.

The following accounts are actual recollections of individuals who have found that, upon reaching their respective points of futility, have decided that there are, indeed, other types of justice other than the "trickle down" brand which is manufactured and doled out by the federal government. These people have also found that their "new and improved" versions of revenge or justice are advantageous in many respects.

For instance, other than divorce court, there is essentially nothing that a person can do when he finds that his spouse is the subject of an extra-marital relationship. (Nothing LEGALLY, that is.) Also, if someone offers drugs or illegal substances or devices for sale to children, the police agencies cannot usually act unless there is actual, physical, and substantial evidence to support the claim. And if a person is on the slightly less than legal side of the system, how does he go about filing a theft report or a complaint that someone stole the motorcycle that he stole from someone else just a week before?

But there are other reasons for taking action to right a wrong, and each of the reasons lie within the effector of the avenging action. Anyone who realizes the justice trap of our current system of government can appreciate the fact that it's redundant for a woman to file rape charges against a man when it's commonly known that the victim will suffer more than the guilty person even if he were found to be guilty! It's simply not worth the effort in many cases to pursue an alleged wrong through the justice system. This goes for many types and classes of crimes where the judicial sentencing is apt to be considerably less than effective.

When the assailant is a legal minor, such as those involved in the gang-rape "wilding" of a New York woman where all of the assailants were juveniles and are representations of the ineffectiveness of the justice system when dealing with juveniles.

I've seen police officers lose their badges for issuing speeding citations to the children of friends or family of public officials, for arresting on charges of burglary the sons of prominent attorneys, as well as other similar reasons. I have heard a very accurate story of a judge who, was found to be trafficking large quantities of cocaine but the only punishment he received was to not be allowed to run for re-election, which was okay because he had already announced his retirement.

Or the account of the judge who's son struck and killed a small child with a motor vehicle while recklessly driving through a residential area at over 60 mph. The judge's son's vehicle was examined by a forensic sciences lab and was found not to have been involved in the incident (although there were numerous eyewitnesses to the incident who could testify otherwise!) This was the same judge who had another son who stabbed a teenager in the chest killing him instantly, with no other provocation than a few misplaced words. This son was forced to enlist in the armed forces but was released a few weeks later with a general discharge. It seems as though the punishment was to merely enlist in the service, with nothing said about remaining for any specified period of time.

There is information of a Sheriff who owns a marijuana farm which was taken over from a dealer and manufacturer who would not play the games of the Sheriff. A Sheriff who's deputies allegedly removed a case of stolen automatic pistols (and other evidence) from the scene of a drug bust and kept for their own personal use. Naturally, there was insufficient evidence for legal action to be taken or even processed. This is the same system who allegedly employs a man in the capacity of probation officer who distributes pornographic material and consequently seduces and molests the juvenile boys under his supervision.

The point I'm trying to make is that these things happen around us on a daily basis because the system is imperfect. Therefore, there is a need for persons to know how to take care of their own and rely less upon the legal system for protection. Such is the story of a gentleman (who wasn't without influence) who lost his son to the bullet of a known drug dealer and convicted felon.

Over a period a several weeks, the police department stated in their repertoire of excuses that, even though they knew who the guilty party was there was nothing that could be done because there was no tangible evidence with which the killer could be brought to trial. This was in spite of the fact that the killer was heard to laugh and joke about the killing (and others) and it was by his own admission to a police officer that he had, in fact, committed the murder. The admission did not hold up in court, however, due to the fact that it was made before the officer could read the killer his Miranda Warnings prior to the admission of guilt. After a while, things quieted down with the case and everyone seemingly forgot about the murder, with a couple of exceptions, of course.

The plane quietly touched down on the runway under the cover of darkness and rolled up the tarmac until coming to a stop at the port of entry and the customs office. The cargo door opened and two men stepped out carrying the limp profile of a third. They laid the silent and still figure upon the ground, re-entered the plane, and sped off down the runway, disappearing into the darkness from whence they had come.

When the man who had been left behind finally gained consciousness he found himself to be in a very strange and unfamiliar environment. The faces, the smells, the locations, and even the language spoken was unlike anything he had ever heard. It was like awakening from a dream only to be faced with a nightmare.

Word had it that this man was taken from the protection of his home and friends, administered a heavy dosage of sedative, had pouches of cocaine taped to his torso by his assailants then taken to a dark and almost deserted runway in the Middle East (or was it the Far East?) then consequently was found by customs agents of the foreign country. It has also been heard that the subject in question was the very same person who was responsible for the killings of several persons, including one victim who was the son of a very prominent business man. And, further word has it that this man is still in prison in that little out-of-the-way country and will spend the remainder of his life amidst the rats and roaches while he ponders his existence and wonders who it was that got him and for what reason.

Not all stories are of such poetic conclusion but what they lose in poetry, they seem to make up for in imagination. And especially imaginative and intriguing is a variation of the "Big Store" con which has been in operation since the early '30's and still very successful, I might add. The motivation for this came in the form of a young man who had been conned out of a substantial amount of money on a business venture.

Since there was no legal basis for action against the con, the victim decided to take matters into his own hands for retaliation in kind. He began to research his potential target and found several intriguing tidbits of information such as implication in a multi-million dollar money laundering scheme, illegal foreign currency exchange houses, DWI convictions with no jail time served, and implication in religious oriented crimes and cons which would bring in untold millions on an annual basis.

Above all, it was found that the target's weaknesses were alcohol, gambling, and religious efforts to provide children's relief, as well as the fact that the target couldn't turn down a chance to make a fast dollar. After some planning, a letter was drafted and sent to the target, supposedly from a very respected religious organization which stated that the organization was having difficulty in a current venture and were finding it difficult to raise needed money. The letter further stated that the organization had decided to hold a contest, selling chances at $1,000 per entry with the winning entry receiving a certified check for $10,000. The remainder of the proceeds would then go to their specific endeavor.

The strategist knew that the target was inclined to write worthless checks to cover his debts and decided to use this in his favor. He further stated in his letter to the target that the entrance fee could be paid by check.

A week or so passed before the mailman brought the reply to the strategist which was in the form of a personal check in the amount of $2,000 for two chances. The bait was taken. The strategist sat back and waited until a week or so after the deadline of the "contest" had passed, then sent an urgent telegram to the target notifying him that he had won the contest, but that his entrance check had not cleared. It was explained in the telegram that the target could claim his check by the wire-transfer of funds to a specific bank and claim his $10,000 certified check by return wire transfer. The target quickly arranged to clear the check and the money was transferred.

Well, $2,000 of it anyway.

In other events, it's a pretty common concession that certain social classes are somewhat immune from the day-to-day innundations of the problems which seem to plague those of lesser social standing. Cockroaches, for example, seem to be a problem only of the lower classes. Until one day...

For many months, a family had been renting a small, cramped frame house from a vary affluent couple. She was a college professor, he a prominent attorney. The landlords had been promising the family for months the problem they were having with cockroaches would be taken care of immediately, but immediately was always put off until tomorrow and tomorrow never came. Push came to shove and all involved found themselves in front of a small-claims court judge.

Generally, small-claims court does no allow the litigants the luxury of an attorney. The judge simply hears the case and makes a decision in favor of whoever provides the best evidence for his respective argument. Naturally, the landlord won the case due to the fact that there was no written agreement that the landlord was to take care of the roach problem, and the renters would be forced to find their own solution to their problem, at their own expense. And to make matters worse, the landlords raised the rent on the small house to make up for the loss in money and time for having to take off from work and appear in court. This was more than the renters could take.

Over the next few days, the man began to collect roaches from his house, his neighbors' houses, and wherever else he could find the little creatures of the cockroach persuasion. As he collected them, he stored them in a gallon jar until the jar was alive with the insects. It was time to make his play.

The strategist found out that the roaches multiply at an amazingly fast rate when left in cool, dark places, such as inside a 50 pound bag of dog food he had purchased. And by strange coincidence, the brand of dog food he had purchased was the same brand which his landlord fed his own dogs. The strategist made a small incision in the bag and poured several dozen roaches inside, then sealed the bag shut with a stapler. After that, he waited for the right moment.

The day of the offensive quickly came. The strategist knew the working hours of the landlords so he would not be worried about their presence. The trick was to get his collection of creatures into the landlord's house and garage without being seen.

He lucked out with the garage. Upon his arrival, he found that the target had left the garage door standing open, revealing a fresh, 50 pound unopened bag of dog food standing just inside the door. He quickly switched the bags. Then upon further assessing the situation he found that the best way to get the roaches into the target's house was to scale the fireplace wall and pour the jar of critters down into the chimney. Since it was early summer, there was no problem with this approach.

The attorney never knew where the sudden infestation came from but quickly learned that even he was not immune from their hungry little mouths. Perhaps he learned a lesson in humanity as well, or just began to feel more sympathetic towards those who rented his houses, but in either case he conceded to have all of his properties exterminated not once, but on regular intervals. Including his own house and office.

I guess the moral of the story is that a person can always make the landlord change his ways, especially if he bugs him enough! Well, at least the problem wasn't skunks.

And there is another saying which pertains to the following situation: paybacks are a bitch!

A police officer I know quite well once recounted an incident which pertained to a lady who was divorced and had been granted a house which she and her ex-husband had shared since their marriage. The only problem was that with the house, she also had a severe problem with a group a boys who occupied the house next door to hers.

Actually, the boys resided in a large, unsightly recreational vehicle that was parked in their yard most of the time. Therein lay the biggest part of the problem.

The boys had the habit of connecting their RV, via an electrical extension cord, to the young lady's house with which they supplied electricity for their air conditioner, microwave, television, and other electrical appliances which were used for their front-yard camping excursions. After the event, they would toss their trash next door, including beer and whisky bottles and used condoms.

She had tried calling the police but found there was nothing that they could do due to the fact that each time they were called out to investigate the complaint, the electric line would be quickly disconnected before they could arrive. One officer was very sympathetic, however, and offered the lady some "off the record" advice. She listened intently as he told her of a plan.

A day or so later an electrician's van pulled up to her house, an electrician disappeared into the garage for a while, then came out and drove away. As he left, he commented in a loud voice that he would have to come back the following week to complete the job, so that the next door neighbors could hear the conversation. As he drove away, the lady walked back to her house followed by a barrage of snickers and laughter from the RV.

Later the same evening as she was sitting in her living room watching television, the lights in her house dimmed a little, followed by a succession of popping sounds and several screams that she had determined to be from her neighbor's camper. She immediately smelled smoke and with the sounds of approaching fire engines decided that she should join others who were appearing in the street to watch the commotion.

The fire trucks and police units arrived and then an ambulance. They all converged upon the neighbor's RV which by now was fully engulfed in flames, as was the house which it sat in front of. While one of the boys had been rushed to the hospital, two others were carried off to jail after they had been spotted while attempting to dump a large quantity of drugs into the bushes.

As the police officer who had helped the lady with her "plan" stood with the other bystanders, he was heard to remark something to the effect that "That's what happens when you plug in a 110 volt appliance into a 220 volt receptacle!"

A person can contrive almost anything if the motivation is right and the proper materials are accessible. After all, necessity is the mother of invention. Someone with a broad mind and a working knowledge of general gadgetry can be a very devious, if not dangerous, individual.

I recently learned of another young lady who worked as a lab technician in a large hospital, who decided to take action against her ex-lover when he attempted to blackmail her into resuming the sexual part of their relationship. He had found out that she had stolen some lab equipment from the hospital and knew that she would immediately lose her job and be prosecuted if her employer ever found out about the discrepancy. She realized that getting fired for something such as that would result in her losing not only her job, but her college grant as well, and would then be precluded from ever entering the medical field again. She would be dogged with a police record for many years to come. There is only one thing that surpasses the fury of a woman scorned, and that's the attorney of a woman scorned. In this case, however, there was no attorney.

She began her retaliatory efforts by concocting a mixture of chemicals which, when mixed with water would become a very foul smelling concoction and would leave behind a very distasteful, musky odor. The chemicals would eventually take on the odor of very cheap perfume with such power and sweetness that it was almost sickening, but that would be several hours after the smell of human defecation passed.

She left her work early and went directly to her ex-lover's house, which was an apartment just off the campus of a major university. Using the key she had retained from her former relationship, she let herself into the front door after first looking around to see if she had been spotted. She knew that she would have to hurry because her target would be in from afternoon classes very soon, so she went right to work.

She went to the bathroom and poured the mixture into the toilet bowl and tank, then emptied the bottle into the sink drain and turned the water faucet on to activate the chemicals. After glancing around the room, she turned off the lights and left the apartment shortly before her ex-lover returned home.

She had planned her technique well and once she returned to her own apartment, knew exactly how the plan would work. She darted into her own apartment, gathered a few things from her dresser and closet, threw them into an overnight bag, then went to a friend's apartment to enlist some "special" services.

She and her friend laughed and planned as they mixed an odor neutralizer which was laced with a goodly amount of chloroform. Her friend agreed to deliver the mixture to the target's apartment with the instructions that it was from the manager's office. She was also to tell the target that the mixture was not only to be poured down the drains, but sprinkled about the room as a room deodorizer. The girl made the delivery then waited downstairs for the strategist to arrive.

Within a few minutes the strategist arrived and both of them waited in the car to give the chloroform time to take effect while they planned the second phase of the operation in between their laughter and giggles.

When they decided it was time, they went back upstairs to find that the target's front door was unlocked and partially opened. The strategist pushed it further open and the overpowering smell of chemicals was almost too much for them. They quickly ran around the place, opening windows and coughing, almost being overcome by the chloroform. After the air had begun to circulate, they went to work on plan B.

They found him lying on the bathroom floor in a pair of blue-jean cut-offs. He wasn't a very big person so they had no difficulty in moving him onto the sofa in the living room. Once there, they started to work. They quickly removed his shorts and underwear, replacing them with a pair of black fishnet stockings, followed by a pair of spiked heel boots. They wrapped a peek-a-boo bra around him and fastened it, then put a Lone Ranger mask on his face. They finished off the outfit by placing a whip in one of his hands, tossing several erotic S&M manuals on the coffee table, then trashed the apartment for the occasion.

The strategist's assistant had gone into the bedroom and stripped the bedding into total disarray and spraying whipped cream onto the sheets and the mattresses. As an afterthought, she pulled down her own jeans and sat in the whipped cream, leaving a distinct impression in the topping on the bed. She then tied some old-fashioned bondage ropes from other sheets in the lined closet, tied them onto the corners of the bed frame then tossed them onto the mattress as well.

The pair then rendezvoused in the living room to admire their handiwork; there was still something missing. After another couple of minutes, the assistant decided exactly what would round off the event.

"Do you mind a little spontaneous creativity?" she asked the strategist.

"Be my guest!"

That was all she needed. She remembered seeing a feather taped to the mirror in the bedroom and quickly retrieved it, bringing back into the room a tube of super-glue and a laundry marker as well. She sat down in front of the ex-lover and carefully made sure that he had an erection, then drew a smiley-face on it with the laundry marker. She then dropped a few drops of glue onto the shaft of the feather and secured it to the underside of the penis. After an outburst of laughter, the strategist decided to carry the set-up one further by super-gluing the target's hand to the shaft of his penis as well.

They turned the lights down low, removed some wine glasses from the cupboard and filled them with chocolate milk, turned the stereo onto a country and western station, increased the volume considerably, then left the apartment with the front door still partially opened as they had found it.

As the pair hurriedly walked to their cars, they laughed and shared the vision of the target showing up at the emergency room of the hospital, asking the on-duty nurse if she could help him while pointing to his hand which was super-glued to his penis with a large blue feather protruding. By the time they reached their cars, they were almost in hysteria. They looked back up the stairs to see several doors begin to open and faces peering out to see where the noise was coming from.

They decided that it was time to leave the area when the strategist was almost spotted by a person who knew her and the target. The pair quickly drove away. Their only regret was that as an afterthought, they had not taken photographs to send out as Christmas cards to all the target's friends in the event that he didn't get the message.

This incident worked for several reasons even though it violated several basic rules the strategist should follow when planning an attack. The main thing that allowed it to work, however, was the judicial system. For instance, it would have been very embarrassing for the target to have to recount his story in a packed court and in front of a jury, in the wildest notion that he ever was to find out who was responsible. And it would be very weak evidence against the strategist, with her being a perky but very petite young lady who wouldn't weigh 105 pounds soaking wet!

The intimidation and threat of blackmail which the target attempted was totally out of proportion with the expectation of payment from the strategist. Also, the target never counted on the strategist to be clever enough to contrive of such a retaliation, instead he viewed her as a shy, introverted person who wasn't capable of hurting a fly. He trusted in human nature that she would rather succumb to his threats than to retaliate. As I said before, it is never wise to fully trust human nature!

The last account of revenge also pertains to a young college student, in this case a male who was majoring in accounting.

He found himself to be falling behind and having difficulties in keeping up his grades and was put on academic probation for his deficiency. The guarantor screwed up the student's paperwork and though this was the student's first offense, his financial assistance was stopped completely, and a hold was placed on his transcript as well as further assistance.

Because of the lack of funds with which to live on and pay for his books and tuition, the student was forced to take on a full-time job to support himself and soon found himself having to drop out of school altogether.

By sheer luck and coincidence, he found himself working as a teller at the very bank where his loan had originated. And with accounting as a major, he quickly caught on to the work but soon became very bored. To further his quickly deteriorating attitude, he found that his take home pay was substantially less than he had expected, and he was required to immediately begin repaying a portion of his student loan. After making some quick calculations, he decided that it would take him at least three more years before he was financially able to return to college and even complete one semester. And he still needed a year and a half to graduate.

Friday came along and by then he had become very depressed. He took the bus home after work, and as he passed by a church, he noticed a billboard in front of the church which stated they were attempting to raise money for some project. He suddenly had an idea.

By the following Monday morning, he was his old, chipper self again after spending the weekend plotting and planning about his quickly to be acquired wealth. The week went by quickly and on Friday, he had checked the legalities of his plan, provided himself a few loopholes, and put his plan into action. He quickly amassed over $2500 in a period of 24 hours.

By the second week into the plan, his profits had tripled and the wealth had begun to show in his lifestyle.

He began to wear new clothing, sported a new watch and ring, and was soon seen driving around town in a new sports car. This began to raise the suspicions of his supervisors at the bank as well as the bank president, who lost no time in having the new teller's books and cage audited. To their surprise, the teller's books and cash count was the clearest and most accurate in the entire teller department. The president was still not convinced, however, and took the teller out of the cage and put him on a desk and running errands throughout the office building. Within another week, his profits from his venture surpassed even his wildest expectations.

Although the teller was seemingly out of immediate danger, and there was no chance of his handling more money until the president was satisfied with his honesty, the internal security department had begun an in-depth probe into the teller's private life to see if there were any reports of drug dealing or other illegal activity. They found absolutely nothing. As a matter of fact, the teller-turned-strategist was known by all to be of impeccable character. The president was getting very worried and distraught, but there was absolutely nothing that he could do because a crime had not been committed, so all he could do was to sit and wait while the teller got richer.

As it turned out, the wait was very short. The teller drove in to work the following Monday morning driving a top-of-the-line Corvette convertible. The president could take no more. He called the teller into his office and the questioning began. The bank pres was in a slightly different mood, however, in that now he was more curious to know where the money was coming from rather than focusing upon prosecution of the teller. His own greed began to show through.

So the two talked for a while on a man-to-man basis, as opposed to a boss-to-employee basis. As they talked, the president became more and more enthused about the situation.

The teller recounted his decision to supplement his income in a most creative way. He first invested his initial paycheck in a fairly expensive ladies' necklace and sold lottery tickets to the secretaries in the office building with the necklace as a prize. That worked so well that he decided to try a different approach. Instead of giving away necklaces or watches, he decided to give away $100 as the first prize and $20 as a second prize. This was about the time that the president took him out of the teller cage which left him to be able to sell his tickets throughout the entire office building. His clientele quadrupled.

The teller went on to say that he had made so much money off the scheme, that he now had enough money to pay for his entire education, enough to live on for a couple of years, and to purchase the prize for the next raffle to which he had already sold tickets. The prize, of course, was the new Corvette convertible he had driven to work.

The president was no longer really concerned that a law had been violated, he was instead more preoccupied with the possibility of adverse negative publicity if the stockholders and investors ever found out what was going on. He talked to the strategist for a while longer and agreed to let him remain at the bank until after the lottery was over and the prize given away in the final raffle.

The Friday of the raffle came and went. The strategist went on about the business of selecting the winning ticket and presenting the prize. Shortly afterwards, he picked up his final paycheck, said goodbye to all of his past clientele, then drove away.

In this case, the strategist wasn't out to hurt anyone and all he wanted was to be able to pay for his continuing education. He came out of the deal happy, and with a hefty profit from the venture. The secretaries and other clientele were happy because they had pretty much profited from the scheme as well. The president? Well, he came out happy as well, which was very obvious by the smile on his face as he tooled around town in his new Corvette.

The techniques and methods which have been depicted in this chapter are not fictitious: they are actual occurrences which happened to real people. People like you and I who have found ourselves at times to want to choke the crap out of someone who treated us badly. The strategists in this presentation were very imaginative and creative, and illustrate what a person is capable of doing if they are forced into a corner with nowhere to turn. Although these are examples of true-life experiences, they should not be attempted by the amateur strategist. There are many contingencies to consider and stuff such as this should be left to the more experienced person. Remember that any offensive action could result in total disaster for all concerned, and the key is to get even, not fall behind or be trampled underneath!

Conclusion

Throughout this book I have stressed that there is, indeed, a need for alternative capabilities. The reader should allow that, under certain circumstances, all IS fair in love and war! In order to better prepare himself for certain confrontations, he must understand the logistics of his undertaking and must be able to accept full responsibility for his actions, both physically and mentally.

In presenting this material in the manner which it was written, it is hoped that the reader understands the need for introspection as well as situational analysis, but not just in responsive counter attacks. Likewise, a person will live a richer and fuller life if he is more circumspect and allows himself a much broader perspective on life. By following certain philosophical observances, and applying learned techniques, anyone should be able to master their life and be able to effectively confront and control any situation which they may happen to be faced with.

Knowledge, perspective, and utilization are the three most essential elements a person should have. Aside from health, these three things are immediately necessary not only for essential survivability but for an enhanced lifestyle, personal freedom, and the things which can be acquired in life that are not of the basic necessities: the luxuries, the niceties, and the things which pleases our senses.

If everyone accepted their situations as being their destination in life, and if everyone blindly accepted the decisions of those that rule and govern our lives, then there would be no need for books such as this. But then, there would likewise be no need for police organizations, churches, or any other institution which is unique to the free system as we know it. As it is seen, the laws are designed to protect the guilty and to promote the innocent as a marketable commodity. And contrary to popular belief, it isn't the written law which is so insidious in-as-much as the problem lies within the biased and prejudiced intent which lay just beyond control of the people and line the pockets of the rich. The laws are written in such a manner that even their respective authors cannot interpret them, so how can "We, the people..." expect the court justices and policing agencies to interpret the laws correctly? In essence, we cannot.

And there is a punch line to the joke: it is said that the reason the Mafia is losing their grip on organized crime and unscrupulous, underhanded activity is due to their inability to compete with the agencies of the government.

———Notes———

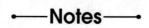

Notes

Other Books Available From Desert Publications